KU-496-986

A Short Guide to Modern British Drama

JOHN RUSSELL BROWN

Associate Director and Repertoire Adviser at the National Theatre of Great Britain

1 160 377 00

HEINEMANN EDUCATIONAL BOOKS
LONDON

Heinemann Educational Books Ltd
22 Bedford Square, London WC1B 3HH

LONDON EDINBURGH MELBOURNE AUCKLAND
HONG KONG SINGAPORE KUALA LUMPUR
NEW DELHI IBADAN NAIROBI KINGSTON
EXETER (NH) PORT OF SPAIN

© John Russell Brown 1982
First published 1982

British Library Cataloguing in Publication Data

Brown, John Russell
    A short guide to modern British drama.
    1. English drama — 20th century — History and
    criticism
    I. Title
    822'.914'09   PR736
    ISBN 0-435-18372-9

822·09

BOROUGH OF BARNET
PUBLIC LIBRARIES

21 JUL 1992

J.M.L.S.

C

Typeset by The Castlefield Press of Northampton
in 11/13 pt Baskerville, and printed in Great Britain by
Biddles Ltd, Guildford, Surrey

Contents

Preface   vii

Part One: New Plays in Britain Since the Second World War
    A New Sense of Reality   3
    Interior Drama   9
    Exploratory Drama   17
    Performance Drama   25
    Well-Made Plays   31
    A Sense of the Present   38

Part Two: Twenty-Five Plays by Twenty-Five Writers
    John Arden   THE WORKHOUSE DONKEY   45
    Alan Ayckbourn   BEDROOM FARCE   47
    Howard Barker   NO END OF BLAME   49
    Samuel Beckett   HAPPY DAYS   51
    Robert Bolt   A MAN FOR ALL SEASONS   53
    Edward Bond   BINGO   54
    Howard Brenton   EPSOM DOWNS   57
    Shelagh Delaney   A TASTE OF HONEY   59
    Michael Frayn   DONKEY'S YEARS   61
    Simon Gray   OTHERWISE ENGAGED   63
    Trevor Griffiths   COMEDIANS   65
    Christopher Hampton TREATS   67
    David Hare   TEETH 'N' SMILES   69
    Ann Jellicoe   THE SPORT OF MY MAD MOTHER   71
    Peter Nichols   PRIVATES ON PARADE   73
    Joe Orton   WHAT THE BUTLER SAW   75
    John Osborne   INADMISSABLE EVIDENCE   77
    Harold Pinter   THE HOMECOMING   79
    Stephen Poliakoff   CITY SUGAR   81

David Rudkin	ASHES	83
Peter Shaffer	AMADEUS	85
Tom Stoppard	JUMPERS	87
David Storey	EARLY DAYS	89
Arnold Wesker	ROOTS	91
Charles Wood	VETERANS	93

Reference Section
Who's Who: notes on those whose views are quoted, and
  a select bibliography   95
Index to Plays   99
Index to Playwrights   101

Preface

The years since the Second World War have seen a great renaissance of British Drama. A succession of writers have found that they can express themselves most completely and engagingly in the theatre. They have been associated with a wide variety of companies and drawn on the talents of many actors, directors and designers.

This book is written as a guide to the plays of this period. It maps out a tangled terrain, presents individual works of special interest and provides authoritative insights — many from the authors themselves — together with much useful information. I hope it will encourage people to see more performances and follow future developments with keener pleasure.

It is planned as a companion-book for John Goodwin's *Short Guide to Shakespeare's Plays*. But it deals with many authors rather than one and so I have divided it into two parts. The first distinguishes six kinds of drama: it gives a wide view that 'places' the work of some fifty writers and considers the influences at work in the British theatre. The second part presents twenty-five modern plays, by twenty-five authors.

Acknowledgements

In Part I of this book I have drawn on a series of eight talks I gave on Radio 4 in 1981, called *Up to Now: Drama*; I have used this material with the kind permission of the British Broadcasting Corporation.

John Russell Brown

Because of what happened in the fifties we have a band of writers we couldn't have hoped for in 1954.

But any theatre must always seek to widen its audience . . . the doors must be open all day.

Peter Hall

Part One

New Plays in Britain
Since the Second World War

A New Sense of Reality

Back in the 1930s, successful new plays varied little in form. A group of people talked and moved around in a replica of a living-room, bedroom, restaurant, or other recognisable setting. Their talk was animated and distinctive, and the décor was usually elegant, grand or interestingly decayed. During the progress of a play the characters coped with intruders, disasters, mistakes, or revelations about themselves and their pasts, and by the end all was peaceful again. This was fine for audiences who wanted to hold on to their place in the world or to discover a new refuge, and so, for some time after the Second World War, plays written to this formula continued to attract audiences.

J. B. Priestley's *An Inspector Calls*, that had its first production in 1946, is a notable example of this staple drama, with a strong and quietly resourceful intruder entering a family circle. T. S. Eliot's *The Cocktail Party* of 1949 was basically old-fashioned — the characters all friends together — but the dialogue was in verse rather than prose and the alien figure was a mysterious psychiatrist. Terence Rattigan's *Separate Tables* of 1954 was quite regular except that it offered two one-act plays in the place of a single entertainment. Even Robert Bolt's *Flowering Cherry* of 1957, a first play by a new dramatist, followed the standard pattern, varied only by a setting which changed, from a suburban house in London to a cherry orchard in full bloom.

Radical alternatives were few. Some European and American plays provided quite different kinds of drama, but these and the still rarer innovatory British works were confined almost entirely to a few Art Theatres or to amateur companies; and they played to tiny audiences.

The first unmistakeable change came with a play that in many respects ran true to the old form — John Osborne's *Look Back in Anger*, first seen at the Royal Court Theatre, London, in May 1956. All its action takes place in an attic flat and the characters belong to one small group; and in the end there is the usual reconciliation. But the energy of the play's hero Jimmy Porter, expressed in violent and blazing speech, almost bursts the seams of the play apart: *The Guardian*'s critic, Philip Hope-Wallace, called it 'frenzied preaching in an empty conventicle'. John Barber of The *Daily Express* said that the play's hero poured out a 'vitriolic tirade' against the world in wild and whirling words. Besides, the setting was neither elegant nor the natural habitat of the characters: it represented a world from which its inhabitants sought to escape, and they sometimes paced up and down or stood still in mute defiance. *Look Back in Anger* impressed the critics, but its rebellious tone exasperated most of them, and so praise for vitality was matched by reproof for disorderly conduct. It is much easier to see now that a dramatist had arrived who had put what he knew and felt into a play. The individual reality of his characters had come before the customary requirements of theatre. *Look Back in Anger* was herald of many plays that took even more liberties. A new sense of reality swept all restrictions away. When the standard form of the thirties and forties is used after 1960, the dramatist has adopted it, by his choice, for practical reasons.

It is no accident that Jimmy Porter is first seen reading the Sunday papers and that he talks about T. S. Eliot, Vaughan Williams, America, *Ulysses*, Emily Brontë, André Gide, Dante and a host of fashionable cultural idols, new social distinctions and potent political issues. The reality of living had moved ahead of theatrical clichés, and Osborne was raising topics that could achieve present awareness. Politically, intellectually and socially it was a

4

changing world. Already the novel, poetry, music, painting and architecture had broken free from earlier conventions and found distinctive twentieth-century forms and styles. In other countries, change had also come to the theatre, but not in Britain. Only now — in 1956 — John Osborne's play showed that modern drama could make its bid for life.

A new sense of reality was perhaps the strongest agent of change. Already the visual realism of film and the recorded voices of radio had given audiences a taste of actuality that could make the conventional pretences of theatre look very foolish and cumbersome. Certainly these electronic media, and also television once that became fully established, have had a large effect on the plays that have been written since 1956.

Arnold Wesker's *The Kitchen*, first performed in 1957 and seen in London at the Royal Court in 1959, has a single setting in the old style, but not a small manageable group of characters all involved in a single development. Wesker had been a student at the London School of Film Technique and, in his first play, he put on stage what a film camera might have recorded if it had visited the kitchen of a large London restaurant. There is a huge cast and only fragments of plot. Introducing the text, Wesker wrote that 'the world might have been a stage for Shakespeare but to me it is a kitchen, where people come and go and cannot stay long enough to understand each other and friendships, love and enmities are forgotten as quickly as they are made'. The climax of Part One is, simply and boldly, the service of meals for 2,000 off-stage people; some 40 actors are on stage and in the last moments seventeen characters speak in rapid succession, using only a few words at a time.

Wesker had had the courage to write from his own experience — he had, himself, been a pastry cook — and not according to any formula about what makes a good play: his sense of reality came first. This is basic to his work: 'I only feel compelled to bring things together into a play or a story after something has happened to me; it's experience which drives me to write'. Later on, other writers were still bolder in bringing actuality on to the stage. David Storey was both novelist and filmscript-writer before he became a dramatist. His plays often centre on real-life activity; *The Changing Room* shows a rugger team, *The Life Class* shows students and model at an art school. In 1969 *The Contractor* was performed at the Royal Court, staged by Lindsay Anderson, a director practised in film-making. In some ways this is an old-fashioned drama showing two groups of people in a single setting: Mr Ewbank hires and installs marquees and his daughter is getting married. But while the family copes with this change in their lives, we see the Contractor's men erect, decorate and then dismantle the marquee very much as they would on any job. It is this second action that gives shape to the three act play, and its skilled, routine and almost silent work counter-points traditional drama. Its completion brings a quiet but reliable and shared pleasure, a sharp contrast to the personal events which tend to isolate individuals, and leave them unsatisfied. The empty marquee, the decorated, beflowered marquee, the marquee left in disorder after the reception, and the marquee dismantled and fitted into its various bales and coils of rope, are all powerful visual images that provide a touchstone of reality.

In the late sixties, Storey was breaking new ground, but in the 1980s a dramatist starts writing with almost all the freedom of a filmscript-writer. He shows us what happens here, there and almost everywhere, whatever he thinks is relevant to his story or theme. There is no confinement to one or two settings; years pass or go backwards at will, oceans are crossed, wars erupt and generations die. Film

techniques of cutting abruptly from scene to scene
fading from one to another, changes of focus, time, pi
or reality, very short scenes with scarcely a word spoken,
huge silences — all these occur in plays. Many dramatists
believe that this best represents our present sense of
reality; and many of them work in films and TV, so that
they know how to create in this way. Sometimes they
seem to forget basic theatrical necessity and often they
make difficulties for directors, designers and actors. But by
these means they have brought back a sense of surprise,
shock or revelation, qualities that belong to most great
drama.

Howard Brenton is one of the dramatists who have
worked in this way. His *Weapons of Happiness*, first performed at the National Theatre in 1976 is set mostly in
and around a potato-chip factory in London, but suddenly,
with fierce change of light, the stage is a prison cell in
Czechoslovakia. A little later it is a snow-covered street in
Moscow, and then a reception hall in the Kremlin. Before
the end of Act One, it is the London Planetarium and over-
head the galaxies seem to move in their courses. The dramatist has related a local political action to Eastern European
realities and to our sense of being a part of a universe. At
the end of *Weapons of Happiness*, Howard Brenton takcs
the action into yet another sphere when the stage becomes
an orchard in rural Wales in the depths of winter, and quite
deserted. The farmer has gone bankrupt and left his home-
stead. Five characters from the play arrive at the end of a
journey; three go off at once to rummage for something to
eat, and the other two stay only long enough to decide
that they cannot stay, but must return to life in a city.
Twenty-five years earlier, when elaborate constructions of
scenery were 'built' on stage, such a last minute and short-
lived change would have been condemned as impracticable
and unsettling to the progress of a play in its vital last

7

moments. Today, theatre technicians are used to such changes, and the dramatist's requirement is recognised as essential because it allows the argument of his play to be extended and its relevance widened.

David Edgar's *Destiny* which opened at the Aldwych Theatre, London in 1977 is another example of the new open-style realism. It starts by showing the break-up of British rule in India, and then moves to the Midlands of England where an ex-soldier starts an antique business, gets taken over by big business and then joins a new Fascist political party. It is a prophetic play about what might happen in England: it claims the theatre's right to present large issues, and uses its ability to catch an audience's attention by a sense of present reality. In a Radio 4 interview, its author said that by such techniques plays could 'move into the great areas of public life', including industrial and political subjects. He also stressed that theatre works best when an audience can 'find something to recognise' in what happens on stage.

In the 1980s British drama is able to be uninhibited, inventive, and ambitious; it can stimulate and clarify our sense of being alive. But not all new plays are good. More is at risk when so much is possible, and perhaps that is why only a few of the great number of plays premiered each year can command large audiences or show signs that they will live beyond their first productions.

Interior Drama

> He was incapable of recording surface. . . . The copiable he does not see. He searches for a relation, a common factor, substrata. Thus, he is less interested in what is said than in the way in which it is said. . . .
>
> Thus 'you are charming' equals 'it gives me pleasure to embrace you'.

Samuel Beckett's comments on Marcel Proust's great novel *A la Recherche du Temps Perdu* were written in 1931 and show that already, by that time, he possessed the understanding of interior life existing below spoken thought which was to inform his first play, *Waiting for Godot*. Written in French in 1948—9, this 'tragi-comedy' was first performed in Paris in 1953; a London production followed at the small Arts Theatre in 1955, in a translation by its Irish-born author. At rehearsals of a later revival, Beckett said that every important statement in this play 'may be taken at three or four levels'. Only the simplest words and sentence structures are used, but the dialogue is memorable and claws at our minds. Balance and shape give it authority, and the crucial silences and repetitions help the few words to suggest great subtextual pressures that exist below their surface, in the substrata. The characters do not tell us all, like the players in *Hamlet* who cannot 'keep counsel': but Beckett's economy, control and sense of humour help us to *sense* everything, and to discover all for ourselves.

The setting of *Waiting for Godot* is 'A country road. A tree. Evening.' The effect is simple, but eloquent. The characters stand, sit or move on ground where a road has been built, presumably going somewhere and coming from somewhere; a journey seems possible, and at times necessary.

The tree marks a particular location and represents another form of life. 'Evening' means that night and darkness are coming, although each Act of the play ends with a rising moon.

The action is what happens when two tramps, Estragon and Vladimir, wait for Godot, someone who will come — or so they say — and who might change their lives. This waiting is diversified by two visits, one in each Act, of a master and his servant, Pozzo and Lucky; these two come and go, caught up in the business that holds them together and in the misadventures that they encounter. There is also a boy — or possibly two identical boys — who seems to bring a message from Godot saying that he will not be coming this day.

From these few elements Beckett wrote a play that has captured imaginations throughout the world and is already hailed as the greatest 'classic' of postwar theatre. Anyone who has seen a performance will know that its simplicity is deceptive; an audience is led towards Beckett's sense of what it is like to be conscious of one's self and of one's own uncertainties. Estragon seems to represent the feeling faculty of consciousness, Vladimir the intellectual. The setting becomes increasingly suggestive, so that a reference to the tree illuminates the way we search for significance in nature, or in a symbol — the 'tree of life' — or how we take refuge from feeling in being able to name an object; and also how a chance observation can suggest a new diversion:

ESTRAGON: And if we dropped him? (*Pause.*) If we dropped him?

VLADIMIR: He'd punish us. (*Silence. He looks at the tree.*) Everything's dead but the tree.

ESTRAGON (*looking at the tree*): What is it?

VLADIMIR: It's the tree.

ESTRAGON: Yes, but what kind?

VLADIMIR: I don't know. A willow.

> *Estragon draws Vladimir towards the tree. They stand motionless before it. Silence.*

10

ESTRAGON: Why don't we hang ourselves?
VLADIMIR: With what?
ESTRAGON: You haven't got a bit of rope?
VLADIMIR: No.
ESTRAGON: Then we can't.

Silence.

VLADIMIR: Let's go.

Criticism can make *Waiting for Godot* sound pretentious, but in performance it is invigorating and adventurous. Its action is varied by fights, mock fights, comic routines, verbal exercises to sharpen the mind, and various attempts at entertainment; there are also desperate gestures and comic mishaps. The characters are often aware of themselves as performers and laugh at their own pretensions. Sometimes the speeches are sustained, as when Vladimir or Pozzo try to respond eloquently to human suffering or to the beauties of twilight, and, most notably, when Lucky, the clown-like servant, is told to 'think' — then a tirade comes streaming forth until it is forcibly stopped.

When *Waiting for Godot* was performed in London one year before John Osborne's *Look Back in Anger*, it seemed like a play from another world. It came from Paris which was then the centre of *avant garde* theatre, with Ionesco's absurdist plays breaking all realistic tenets to present a crazy, yet purposeful, fantasy world where characters might have several noses, chant nonsense, imitate railway trains, fly in the air or duplicate themselves and where a corpse could grow until it was much longer than the stage was wide. Besides *Waiting for Godot* was by a practised writer who was more than twenty years older than the innovatory British dramatists and had an authority that they did not. For these reasons, Beckett's play became a landmark, signalling a freedom to innovate which others had to reach along their own routes.

Ann Jellicoe (*Sport of My Mad Mother*, 1958), N. F. Simpson (*One Way Pendulum*, 1959) and Heathcote Williams (*AC/DC*, 1970) are writers who have moved far away from ordinary stage illusions or realistic portraiture. Their plays were dubbed 'experimental' by the critics and perhaps there was some accuracy in this, for none of them has had an extended career as a dramatist.

Harold Pinter, born in Hackney in 1930, has proved the most adventurous of the innovatory dramatists who started their careers in the late fifties. His first plays, *The Room* (1957) and *The Birthday Party* (1958), puzzled the critics and found appreciative audiences in universities, rather than in the West End or regional repertory theatres; and since that time he has continued to move ahead of expectations. He has been wary, tenacious and honest in the pursuit of a drama that invites us to see below the surfaces of life and beyond the limits of immediate perception — and a drama that entertains us too.

Pinter has said that he finds it very difficult to analyse his own work and he seems to be engaged in a probe or exploration. But, whereas Beckett expresses his own consciousness of life, Pinter starts with the observation of others and creates a living image in which those characters reveal themselves progressively. Beyond that he has no purpose, as he explained in a radio interview:

> I don't come on at the end of the play and explain the whole thing to the audience. . . . I don't think the theatre is a place to sermonise and if anyone wants to give over an explicit point of view, they can always go to a political meeting or the Church, stand on a soap-box and say it, or write an essay in a magazine. But theatre is — should be — a living moment, something that's happening then and is self-explanatory. What it means is what it says, and what the characters say.

Harold Pinter writes with a control and subtlety that are like Beckett's, and an audience responds with a similar awareness of subtext, or substrata, behind the words that are spoken. Encouraged perhaps by his training as an actor, Pinter is especially conscious that a character on stage, like a human being, communicates by other means than his words as they might be written down; sometimes a casual listener to his plays might think that no communication is taking place. A developing ability to use this level of expression, below the surface of words, led to a series of plays that give a new and heightened perception. As Constable or Cezanne taught their contemporaries to look at nature afresh, so Pinter offers a new way to look and listen, a keen and probing awareness that does not disappear after the fall of the curtain.

Pinter's plays are original, but they also draw upon many long-established and basic arts of the theatre. One of the hallmarks of his writing are silences and the strength of these may derive in part from his knowledge of Chekhov and Shakespeare, and from his appreciation of grand acting in a tradition reaching back to the nineteenth century. As an actor, he had performed minor roles in the late Sir Donald Wolfit's classical repertory company, and he has retained vivid impressions of the 'savagery and power' of some of this actor-manager's long silences and large gestures. He had also acted in small repertory companies and could appreciate at first hand the finesse of Noël Coward's social comedies and the holding power of plot in Agatha Christie's thrillers. Attention is gripped in his early plays when an intruder comes and questions someone who had considered himself safe and on home territory.

In *The Caretaker* of 1960, Pinter's first long-running success, a sense of menace comes from an act of apparent hospitality and generosity. Aston lives in a room in an empty house, but at first the audience sees another man alone in that room. He says nothing and leaves as soon as he hears the sound of people approaching; and then Aston enters with Davies, a tramp, and it is clear that they have seen nothing of the other man. Aston tries to make his visitor feel at home, but something is wrong, and Davies does not dare to sit down on the chair that is offered:

ASTON: Sit down.
DAVIES: Thanks. (*Looking about.*) Uuh. . . .
ASTON: Just a minute.

> ASTON *looks around for a chair, sees one lying on its side by the rolled carpet at the fireplace, and starts to get it out.*

DAVIES: Sit down? Huh . . . I haven't had a good sit down . . . I haven't had a proper sit down . . . well, I couldn't tell you . . .
ASTON (*placing the chair*): Here's a chair.
DAVIES: Ten minutes off for a tea-break in the middle of the night in that place and I couldn't find a seat, not one. All them Greeks had it, Poles, Greeks, Blacks, the lot of them, all them aliens had it. And they had me working there . . . they had me working. . . .

> ASTON *sits on the bed, takes out a tobacco tin and papers, and begins to roll himself a cigarette.* DAVIES *watches him.*

All them Blacks had it, Blacks, Greeks, Poles, the lot of them, that's what, doing me out of a seat, treating me like dirt. When he comes at me tonight I told him.

> *Pause.*

ASTON: Take a seat.
DAVIES: Yes, but what I got to do first, you see, what I got to do, I got to loosen myself up, you see what I mean? I could have got done in down there.

At least two of the three characters in *The Caretaker* are potential killers and their varying manoeuvres keep attention so taut that danger can be sensed, even as they make efforts to reassure themselves and each other.

Soon after this, Pinter started to write in another style, closer to Coward and classical comedy. *The Collection*, produced for television in 1961 and the following year staged at the Aldwych Theatre, is a tightly organised play about four people variously connected with the fashion trade and elegant living. Television's ability to change location easily

14

and rapidly is used in the stage version to awaken the audience's sense of incongruity and to heighten the comedy. Speeches are often more fluent than in earlier plays but in their highest flights they can reveal more and more of a speaker as he warms to a theme and so undermine the effect that he is trying, consciously, to create. Such dialogue is gratifying to perform and communicates on several levels.

There is seldom much plot in Pinter's plays: their characters are few in number, and their settings are often unchanging. In a sense the whole play is an exposition, so that by the end all the potential movements and encounters of a basic situation have been completed and the audience has reached the end of a journey of discovery. All movement comes to a halt during the final moments and the play becomes a silent tableau. It is like watching a game of chess, where all the last moves are inevitable.

Pinter has had many imitators, but no competitor has come within sight. The surface characteristics of his style can be copied easily enough, but not the subtle, stealthy and imaginative involvement that is the basis of his art. Perhaps because of this, Pinter's achievement, like Beckett's, has had a liberating influence. Many British dramatists from 1960 onwards have gained new impetus to explore their own ways of breaking the surface of appearances and showing the reality of our inner worlds.

After *The Homecoming* of 1965, Pinter has written fewer full-length stage plays, but each one of them marks a new departure. *Old Times* of 1971 is about memories of youth in middle-age and shows a man, successful in his career, being 'crass' and helpless before a gentle, clear-eyed and self-reliant woman. This sensitive and haunting play is also one of Pinter's wittiest.

No Man's Land of 1975 presents two poets in their sixties and is a first treatment of what it is like to be a writer. Hirst is successful and lives with a support-system of two servants and plenty of alcohol. Spooner is unsuccessful, and lives by undertaking all kinds of literary activity. Late one night, Hirst has brought Spooner to his home and, in reply to his guest's ready conversation, asks if he speaks 'with a weight of experience behind him'. Spooner replies:

> And beneath me. Experience is a paltry thing. Everyone has it and will tell his tale of it. I leave experience to psychological interpreters, the wet dream world. I myself can do any graph of experience you wish, to suit your taste or mine. Child's play. The present is truly unscrupulous. I am a poet. I am interested in where I am eternally present and active.

In that speech the character seems to voice some of his author's aspirations. Hirst can say nothing in reply: a stage direction indicates that he stands, goes to the drink cabinet, and pours himself a vodka.

Betrayal of 1978 is a love-story, but presented backwards. The audience is led to hear Jerry's first avowal of love in the play's last moments so that not only the joy and strength of his words are understood, but also their helplessness. The three characters are all engaged in imaginary worlds — in their loves, and also in their work where they exploit the products of other people's imaginations: Jerry is a literary agent, Robert a publisher, and Emma, as her marriage becomes insecure, starts an art gallery. As they heighten and intensify their lives by exploiting imagination, betrayals are both complicated and painful. This play is beautifully crafted so that it reveals innumerable nuances of thought and feeling. Moreover, it provides wonderful parts for three actors and encourages the kind of attention in an audience that can appreciate those performances. The critic John Peter said, on BBC Radio's *Kaleidoscope*, that, at one moment in the first production, Penelope Wilton as Emma 'absolutely filled the whole theatre' with 'a facial expression' — a silent, wounded face, 'suggesting a small and hurt animal'.

16

Exploratory Drama

John Arden's *Serjeant Musgrave's Dance*, first performed at the Royal Court Theatre, London in 1959, is written in a bold, clear and energetic style. Characters speak as if they want to give evidence, confident in their attitudes; when they are uncertain, they say so. It is in bold contrast to the new realistic plays of the late 1950s by Osborne, Wesker and Pinter. Instead of providing pictures of contemporary life and making them ring true, John Arden creates models of life, with actions, dialogue and characters all sharper, stronger and more exciting than anything life-like. Often he chooses historical subjects and so avoids direct comparisons with everyday reality.

Serjeant Musgrave's Dance is a play about war and violence. It sets out a variety of attitudes and actions, plain for all to see. Arden has no 'answer' to violence in society, but a story to tell that catches the audience's attention and awakens conflicting reactions. Contrasts are strong because the action moves from one confrontation to another, each one clearly defined. In this way the dramatist explores what violence is and what it can do; he also shows what a desire to have done with it may achieve.

The play is set at the end of the nineteenth century. An army serjeant and three deserters have been horrified at the killings of civilians in a British Protectorate where they have been stationed. One of their fellow soldiers was stabbed in the back and killed, and now they are bringing back his skeleton to his home town in the snow-covered hills of Yorkshire; they intend to display it and so awaken the public to the horror of war. Serjeant Musgrave burns with moral fervour and tries to lead his men with iron discipline.

17

They pretend that they have been sent to enlist new recruits, but all the time they are working towards a public meeting. When this point in the narrative is reached Serjeant Musgrave and his men train a machine-gun on the theatre audience and make them listen to an account of the horrors of war as if they were the townspeople of the play.

As Arden knew very well, his basic technique as a dramatist looks back to the mediaeval theatre, with its strong images, explicit dialogue, schematic characters and moral purpose. It is also in line with the plays of Bertolt Brecht who had developed his own 'Epic' style of theatre in the years between the two wars. Brecht wrote and directed theatre parables, narrative plays that represented the political issues of the day in clear and challenging terms. After the war he was established in East Berlin with a richly subsidised permanent company and his productions reached new standards for socially responsible and brilliantly executed theatre. Instead of involving spectators in an entertaining substitute for their own lives, Brecht sought to awaken members of the audience to observe, to sit in judgement and to think. He did not want them to lose themselves in a thrilling fantasy, but to come to their own conclusions about the varied, conflicting and often very funny pictures of human activity that were displayed clearly in his plays. Instead of working slowly towards one unified effect in a mighty climax, Brecht developed each scene for its own sake so that contrasts between them were as great and surprising as possible; by this means the audience was encouraged to seek out the reasons for what it had witnessed.

It is too simple to say that John Arden was Britain's first Brechtian playwright. The passionate advocacy, celebratory pleasure and romanticism of his writing run counter to the more deliberate dialectic of the German theatre. Arden had also learned a great deal from comic

18

dramatists, the Greek Aristophanes and the Elizabethan Ben Jonson. But Brecht's influence is there, and it proved contagious. Here was an alternative to thorough-going realism of various kinds, and to imaginative escape; a theatre that could be dynamic, intelligent, robust, and true to the essentials of life. Brecht was so influential that the most convincing writers to work in this vein have been careful to mark their disagreements.

In Britain, Edward Bond has by far the most sustained output of the playwrights in this tradition. He has called Brecht the 'great liberator' because he restored to writers the whole world as their subject: it was his plays that showed him that there was no need to write about the 'little things' any more. But in a radio interview of 1971, Bond said that many of the things that he seeks in the theatre are 'specifically anti-Brecht'. He does not believe that it is 'enough just to have people in the theatre to make them think'; the audience's emotions must be involved as well, because that is the way to challenge them most thoroughly.

Bond's first plays to be produced were *The Pope's Wedding* at the Royal Court Theatre in 1962, and *Saved* at the same theatre three years later. Both present scenes of contemporary life and their dialogue represents the ordinary speech of uneducated and unprivileged people. But they challenge audiences by sharpness of focus, taut, unliterary speech and, above all, contrasts between scenes. In Brechtian fashion, each episode in the story is presented in its own terms; the immediate concerns of the characters are never falsified by old theatrical tricks, like inessential verbal eloquence, elaborate by-play or moral comment.

The central characters in *Saved* are a man and wife who have stopped speaking to one another except for mutual accusations. Their daughter, Pam, lives for casual sex and has an unwanted baby. Len has been brought home by Pam and stays on as a lodger, trying to care for Pam and

19

for the baby who might, just possibly, be his. Most scenes are in these people's home, but others show Len's mates meeting in public places with little to do except seek outlets for their instinctive resentments. Violence is a strong undercurrent throughout the play, and it breaks out most appallingly in a scene in a park where young men stone Pam's baby to death in its pram, almost casually as a kind of dare. The last scene is remarkable in another way. It is an almost silent episode in the home; the husband is doing the pools and the women are sitting around and uncommunicative. Len, however, is mending a broken chair; no-one pays any attention when he asks for a hammer — those are the only words in the scene — and so he finishes the job as best he can without one.

An audience's response to this play will change from laughter and perhaps scorn, to horror, concern, despair, and then, surely, to wonder as Len continues to try to care for others and to make peace. His actions make this an optimistic play, despite its bleak, relentless exploration of how the other characters live. Its objectivity and the challenge it makes to an audience to understand the lives of others were to be the distinctive marks of all Bond's later work. He wants to create a 'Rational Theatre' which tries to understand the present day crisis in world affairs and human history and to show the potential for achieving a sane society.

Edward Bond is greatly gifted as an inventor of stories whose actions explore major social issues. *The Woman*, first produced at the National Theatre in 1978 and subtitled 'Scenes of War and Freedom', is set in the times of the Trojan War, but it does not keep to the old stories. It is packed with newly invented incidents. The opening reports that Priam, King of Troy, is dead and shows the frenetic happiness of the Greeks at the death of this fellow man. Image succeeds image, dramatic pictures of the barbarities of

20

war, each one exploring entrenched attitudes and displaying new manoeuvres of cunning, stupidity and greed. At the centre of the most remarkable scenes is Queen Hecuba, and for her, especially, Bond goes far beyond the naked realism of his early plays, commanding an eloquence that seems to stem not from the author but from the speaker's intelligence and feeling. After a hard, passionate sense of outrage in the first half of the play, blind Hecuba, years afterwards, on an island refuge, is given a visionary speech that rises into lyrical verse; this is not verbal elaboration but speech deep-set within the movement of the story and the sinews of the character. It is poetic, because it is true to the moment, precise, and fully and boldly imagined.

Edward Bond is a great fabricator: he has invented and constructed a long series of model worlds for the stage, in which he explores what he calls 'the problems of our culture'. They are solid, tangible, responsible myths, for our times, which challenge the expectations of an audience. The Trojan War has no Wooden Horse, and instead of Helen for whom Homer's heroes fought, Bond has provided a senseless statue of the Goddess of Victory, an emblem and talisman that has no practical purpose whatever. He has also given the Greeks a new leader, Heros, and invented a wife for him who risks her life to alert men to their criminal folly; later she loses her sanity. While Shakespeare's *King Lear* finds comfort in patience and in endurance of the world's ills and the results of his own tyranny, Bond's reworking of that play (*Lear*, 1971) has the defeated despot die in old age while he is trying to pull down with his own hands the Great Wall which allows the army to dominate and enslave his poeple. Bond keeps his audience alert and invites them to question why each incident comes about. There's a challenge in these plays for actors too, because they have to present their roles with a passionate and

21

objective clarity which matches that of the writing. They have no time to dwell in the feelings of any one moment and they discover that no part of the stage and no episode in the play is free from the closest scrutiny.

Bond's use of the theatre 'to look at the problems of our culture', writing plays that are hard to stage and challenging to the audiences, has been a spearhead for other dramatists. David Hare, Howard Barker, Trevor Griffiths and Howard Brenton are among those who tackle public issues, like Bond and Arden, and like Brecht before them; and they use many of the same strategies.

David Hare's *Plenty* was first performed at the National Theatre, in the author's own production, in 1978. It tells the story of Susan, who has been a secret agent in France during the Second World War and afterwards searches for a similar sense of involvement, comradeship and excitement, perhaps of violence and power, too. Her quest is not fulfilled, but takes her to the verge of insanity. David Hare uses the story to illustrate the history of post-war Britain in a series of visually arresting incidents involving Government, gracious living, cheap living, poverty, commerce, art, sex, family, drugs, the Third World and British foreign policy — a huge range of interests for a single play. Almost all the characters are well-educated and ambitious — Susan finds financial success in advertising — and they are given speeches that are cuttingly accurate about their own feelings and their observation of others. With rare exceptions, human contact draws out spikes of distrust and dislike from both sides. The audience is both held and repelled as the play continues its cool demonstration.

The time-scheme is purposefully disjointed, starting in 1962, then jumping back to 1943 and slowly forward to 1962 again; in the last scene Susan is back in the happiness and plenty of 1946. This unchronological progress accentuates the contrasts between past and present. It also draws

attention to the author's theatrical cunning and so enco
ages a Brechtian objectivity.

Howard Barker has also set plays in the earlier years of
this century, but his invention is freest when he explores
the immediate future. He can then anatomise society in
the form in which he thinks it will develop. *That Good
Between Us*, first staged in 1977 by the Royal Shakespeare
Company at their small London theatre, the Warehouse,
shows Britain in some years' time. A nominally socialist
government has a vigilant secret-service that monitors
political talk and eliminates activities dangerous to the
regime. As in *Plenty*, there is a great variety of incident;
attention switches from the private life of the Minister
responsible for security to a scene in a pub and to the
army in action, and then out to sea where a secret agent
dies by drowning. The plot has the tension of a thriller,
but is arrested again and again as the focus narrows on individual dilemmas. Howard Barker catches and challenges
the attention of the audience but also, at crucial moments,
invites them towards empathetic sympathy.

Trevor Griffiths does not use such a wide scope. Although he has written long narrative serials for TV, he
chooses a small focus for the theatre. In *The Party* of 1973,
he brought all his characters together into one room and in
that narrow confine set various political attitudes over
against each other by having them talked out by represent-
ative characters. He uses highly charged encounters to probe
deeply into the grounds for ideas and action.

While other dramatists work consistently in developing
a particular form of drama, Howard Brenton has written
many different kinds of play, from *Sore Throats* (1979),
presenting only three characters in a single setting, to the
triple narrative of *The Romans in Britain* (1980) which
presents three different territorial invasions and the de-
cline of three societies, to the satirical lampoon play about

23

present-day politics, *A Short Sharp Knock* (1980). What all these have in common is a concern for public issues and a developing control over the theatrical medium. Brenton knows how to simplify and harden the outlines of his drama without simplifying meaning or the individual involvement of his various characters. He packs his punches and surprises, so that the very dynamics of his drama challenges or 'stirs up' an audience. He writes broadly too, in a single play presenting many sections of society: when he brings a policeman on stage, he imagines the people he polices and his follow officers, and also his brother or sister who is not in the force.

Besides an obvious debt to Brecht (he has translated *Galileo*), Brenton has a natural affinity to the Jacobean dramatists, seeking dramatic forms that can be, as he has said, 'both dirty and shining white within the same evening; just horrific and also celebratory'.

Performance Drama

Many dramatists would say that an intention to challenge an audience is arrogant and counter-productive. They work on a different principle, believing that their prime objective is to entertain and by this means to share their deepest consciousness with an audience. They consider pleasure to be its own reward.

Such an attitude is implicit in the way most plays come into existence. As they write, authors imagine their text in performance, in a heightened and pleasurable enactment of life. John Osborne has said that when he is working on a new play he 'sees all the parts being played beautifully by [himself], to perfection'; he was an actor before he was a dramatist and knows what this means. He has also said that he would like to write something for a circus, to get 'a really big enlargement of life and people'. In *The Entertainer* of 1957, Osborne did write about a music-hall performer, Archie Rice, who is shown performing with the support of an orchestra. This does not make for an easy or indulgent play, because Archie also addresses the audience directly to voice his bleak despair. In one scene he celebrates the 'normal' man who makes no fuss and, at the same time, the band plays 'Land of Hope and Glory' and a nude in Britannia's helmet is displayed above him on stage. Entertainment is not always undemanding theatre.

The person who did most to give post-war British Theatre a renewed sense of the pleasures of performance was not a dramatist, but the director Joan Littlewood. In the late fifties and early sixties, her Theatre Workshop Company, based at the Theatre Royal in the East End of London, brought to the West End a series of plays that were written for that company and owed more to vitality of performance than to the individual originality of a writer: plays like Shelagh Delaney's *A Taste of Honey*, Brendan Behan's *The Hostage*, Barry Norman's *Fings Ain't Wot They Used T'Be*.

Joan Littlewood's actors worked steadily on developing their physical skills and they had a strong feeling of being a united company with particular aims and a shared pleasure in their work. During rehearsals they improvised scenes that were not in the author's script in order to fill out their understanding of the characters and situations. They also researched documentary material about the events and people portrayed and so discovered for themselves the reality of their roles and actions. They performed with well-grounded confidence. Joan Littlewood introduced music and almost acrobatic action wherever possible, and evoked, or provoked, striking performances from every member of her casts. When speaking about her work, she used the word 'show' rather than 'play' or 'production'.

The fullest example of Littlewood's work is *Oh What a Lovely War* (1963), published as Joan Littlewood's Musical Entertainment, composed with her fellow artists in Theatre Workshop, London. Striking incidents from the First World War are here acted out by a company of Pierrots – the Merry Roosters – who also sing the Music Hall songs of those days. Photographs are projected at the back of the stage which show the actual faces of the generals at more than life-size, and also the weary, suffering figures of ordinary soldiers. There is also a News Panel on which the main facts are flashed, and the appalling statistics of casualties. Vitality of performance was not the only purpose of *Oh What a Lovely War*: it also arraigned the generals and politicians for their inhumanity.

Entertaining vitality and the pleasures of confident and energetic performance – especially comic performances in the old tradition of Music Hall – were all copied by other directors; and dramatists were quick to take the hint — for example, Ann Jellicoe, Henry Livings, Charles Wood, Peter Nichols, Peter Barnes.

Nichols's play, *The National Health* (1969), deals with sickness, medicine and bureaucracy in Britain. Such a theme could have produced a slow-moving, deeply-felt drama or a very complicated and wearying one, but Peter Nichols catches both the feeling and complication of his subject while setting his characters — patients, nurses and doctors — into brisk and sometimes elaborate action, and his script provides wise-cracking dialogue. Even two patients idling away the time are given words that play artfully with double-meanings, non-sequiturs, comic misunderstandings, climax and anti-climax. The author suggests a musical accompaniment for a production.

The dramatist who has been most consistently aware of his role as entertainer is Tom Stoppard. His plays are cramful of startling, witty, metaphorical and irresistable speeches, and quick-silver repartee. Action leads on from surprise to surprise. His invention is so abundant that an audience may feel it shares the author's own delight in his creative fiction, his performance as playwright.

Stoppard's first success was *Rosencrantz and Guildenstern are Dead*, first seen in a fringe production at the Edinburgh Festival in 1966. It tells the story of the two minor characters from Shakespeare's *Hamlet* and intercuts this with episodes of Shakespeare's play, staged with full theatrical glamour. Stoppard's Rosencrantz and Guildenstern are fluent talkers, comically and dangerously so. On the ship, going to England under orders from Claudius, they try to work out how they stand with regard to their charge, Prince Hamlet. Guildenstern builds up his argument with a rhetorical energy that leads him to a false sense of security until it is deflated by Rosencrantz, and then Guildenstern finishes with a nervous laugh. At this point

27

Hamlet enters: he has been listening and so knows that his life is at stake — and so tension sharpens.

Stoppard is always on his toes, and enjoys taking an audience by surprise. He believes that he has to prevent people from leaving their seats before the entertainment is over: 'My absolute primary aim' he has said, 'is that what I write should be engrossing'. Such an aim brings its own disciplines and discoveries: it requires a free mind working within a disciplined form.

The basic situations of the plays are serious enough: *Travesties*, first produced by the Royal Shakespeare Company in 1975, shows Lenin and his wife in Zurich during the First World War. He is working in the library on a book about Imperialism and he answers the call to go to Russia to take part in the Revolution. James Joyce, writer of the twentieth-century epic novel, *Ulysses*, and a surrealist poet, Tristan Tzara, were also in Zurich at the time and have major roles in Stoppard's play. A librarian gives a long lecture on the origins of the Russian Revolution and there is much debate about art and society. But Stoppard moves lightly through the play's many philosophical issues and focuses attention chiefly on Henry Carr, a minor official at the British Embassy. He had performed Algernon in *The Importance of Being Earnest* and had got into litigation with James Joyce — who was managing the production — about reimbursement for a pair of trousers he had purchased for his costume. Henry Carr is shown as an old man who presents the main action of the play as if he were recreating it in his memory. This device eases the exposition and gives a star actor — John Wood in the original production — the opportunity of switching miraculously from age to youth and back again. Carr has a falsifying memory and one that flatters his own role in the central action. So the audience get a triple vision: an old man trying to make sense of himself and the past; the events in Zurich of which

28

the most significant are the completion of *Ulysses* and the departure of Lenin; and thirdly, amateur efforts to perform *The Importance of Being Earnest*. The last words of the play belong to Old Carr, and in them Stoppard invites an assessment of the roles of artists and activists, and of whatever else is important in life:

> Great days . . . Zurich, during the war. Refugees, spies, exiles, painters, poets, writers, radicals of all kinds. I knew them all. Used to argue far into the night . . . at the Odeon, the Terrasse . . . I learned three things in Zurich during the war. I wrote them down. Firstly, you're either a revolutionary or you're not, and if you're not you might as well be an artist as anything else. Secondly, if you can't be an artist, you might as well be a revolutionary . . .
>   I forget the third thing.

Tom Stoppard writes brilliantly about the insecurities of life and his own instinctive pursuit of something that can be said with some assurance. His activity as an entertainer is a highly disciplined adventure, subject to constant self-criticism. Performance of his plays offers an audience a good time and a sense of discovery: what we think matters, and other people matter; the choices we make are always important, despite the way in which we are often fooled by bewildering circumstances and the complexities of role-playing. Old morals like these are given new, twentieth-century life in a series of plays as various and as quickly moving as minds can think.

A keen sense of the pleasures of performance has led Peter Shaffer to write three plays that depend on story-telling and moments of histrionic power. Shaffer also believes that plays should provide moments that change an audience's understanding by a kind of 'revelation' or trans-figuration. *The Royal Hunt of the Sun* (1964) is a specta-cular account of the Spaniards in South America and of the older civilization which they discovered there. It grips attention and provides splendidly visual confrontations.

Shaffer followed *Royal Hunt of the Sun* with *Equus*

(1973), a play that tells two stories. Firstly that of a psychiatrist who sets out to cure a boy who has blinded six horses in an act of irrational violence: the psychiatrist comes to recognise that, in curing the boy — Alan Strang — he has tamed a response to life that he himself lacks and, in some way, wants to possess. The other story is the re-enactment of the boy's experience. This leads to a powerful climax in the first Act when Alan is naked on the back of his horse, Nugget. The animal is played by an actor in a track-suit and horse-mask, but in performance sound, movement and rhythm, the boy's voice calling to Equus, his imagined God, and the supporting actions and sounds of a chorus of other horses bring an overwhelming theatrical excitement: Alan rises up on the horse's back, cries out like a trumpet and twists about like a flame; and then silence comes and he drops slowly to the floor.

Peter Shaffer's next work, *Amadeus*, opened in 1979, and has crowded theatres on the South Bank, in the West End and around the world. Here he presents Mozart and a rival composer, Salieri: the first is what Shaffer calls a divinely gifted genius and the other a talented and successful mediocrity. Both parts offer actors opportunity to display dazzling virtuosity, and the moments of self-realisation and confrontation are supported by recordings of Mozart's irresistible music. Shaffer has again caught his audience with theatrical magic.

Critics are united in recognising the power of Shaffer's plays in performance. But they are divided on the value of what they dramatise. In favour are most of those who recognise the usefulness of the word 'God'. Against are those who do not, and those who resist capitulation to bold theatricality; these all dismiss the plays as melodramas. This conflict of opinion is not at all surprising because the effect of performance depends upon belief and Shaffer has played for high stakes.

Well-Made Plays

Since the late 1950s there have been no accepted patterns for dramatists to follow. Plays are larger, longer, smaller, shorter, slower, quicker than they have ever been. They are more silent, with whole scenes without words, and more noisy, more theatrical, more intellectual, more surprising; they are also less consistent in themselves. A new writer is seldom told that he is breaking the rules; some critics would say that performance is the only reliable test for a play-script.

But not all dramatists are iconoclasts. Every year some new plays are written in the form that was dominant in the 1940s and early 1950s, and for long before that: a group of people in a life-like setting are challenged by a new arrival or an unprecedented event, and then regroup themselves at the conclusion. With considerable cunning all is presented as if for real and the audience is encouraged to view the stage as if seeing into a room with a missing fourth wall.

The old-fashioned well-made play, for all its confinement and predictability — indeed, because of them — has a concision that can be used to concentrate attention and sharpen effect. It is strongly organised and that can encourage eloquence and comedy. It has a direct relationship to the way people live outside the theatre, and that can encourage timeliness; it also allows an author to awaken intimate echoes in the minds of his audience. The small scale and restricted range of such a play allow individual characters to hold attention and to dominate the entertainment.

Of course, the traditional well-made play had to change with the times, within its own conventions. Back in 1947

John Whiting was writing *Saint's Day*; this play, by an actor turned dramatist, won a Festival of Britain prize, but it had only a very short run when it was produced in 1951. Its domestic action does come to the requisite neat conclusion for all concerned, but only through violence and death, and by awakening a corrosive introspection. The second and third Acts threaten theatrical composure and the critics, faced with a new use for an old recipe, condemned the dramatist.

In later plays, John Whiting broke away from the traditional well-made play, but since his time notable achievements have been secured within that pattern. Joe Orton's first play, *Entertaining Mr Sloane* (1964), follows it almost effortlessly. The setting throughout is the living-room of a small house. The characters are a middle-aged brother and sister, Ed and Kath, their old and querulous father, Kemp, and a young lodger, Mr Sloane, who is the traditional intruder. But these simple elements have been adjusted to the author's purposes: the house is isolated and next to a rubbish dump; the brother does not live at home, but comes and goes in an expensive car; the old father is murdered. It is usual, of course, for characters in a well-made play to be sexually attracted to each other, but Orton manages this speedily and without fuss. As soon as she gets him home, Kath seduces Mr Sloane, who is not unwilling; her brother, Ed, also lusts for him and gains possession by engaging him as chauffeur and indulging his whims. The intruder starts by being very much in command, but after murdering Kemp, he becomes dependent on his two protectors. Besides all these modifications to the traditional pattern, Orton has the characters talk with a devastating mixture of frankness and deceit — often self-deceit — and he provides a series of encounters that explode with comic revelations.

Before his early death in 1967, Joe Orton had written

two other stage comedies, *Loot* and *What the Butler Saw*: one features a detective and a coffin, and the other is set in a psychiatric clinic. The mixture of frankness and fantasy within a precisely managed framework is immediately engaging, and offers unusual adventure. The dialogue is as cool, polished and surprising as that of a classic comedy by Oscar Wilde or George Bernard Shaw. Orton was an actor before he was a dramatist — which may be why the form of his plays is so traditional. — but his special contribution is his challenge to orthodoxy that is contained within the inherited form: he played continually with the audience's expectations, and outreached them.

Simon Gray is another traditionalist. His most successful plays are *Butley* of 1971 and *Otherwise Engaged* that followed a few years later. Both show a small group of characters in a single setting and use this form to establish a central character in the audience's understanding. Both heroes are highly articulate, one a university teacher of English and the other a publisher. Both are obsessed with their success and failure. Ben Butley is the more unexpected achievement. He has left his wife and child, and now lives with an ex-pupil turned lecturer who also shares an office with him at the university. He is mischievous and lazy in his work, and belligerent with everyone he meets. Sometimes he declaims in outrageous nursery-rhymes to cut himself off from responsibility; sometimes he retreats into silence. He confesses in his last lines that he's too old and jaded to teach a student whose interest in the poetry of T. S. Eliot he has casually aroused. Butley is very aware of his own immaturity and destructiveness, and so is the audience; the wonder is that the audience finds that it cares. I think this is partly because the other characters keep their subordinate places, and time is taken to show Butley's unease and the painful honesty that drives him forward. That deeper tension is the heart of the play's hold over an audience: when Butley mocks his students' attempts to write about Shakespeare or T. S. Eliot, and his colleagues' attempts to be scrupulous, the audience can sense that this is because he is still a deeply imaginative man who resents the second-best and the pretence of achievement.

While Simon Gray keeps the focus on a single leading character, Michael Frayn, who has also written a series of lively, well-articulated plays, has used the well-tried formula to explore corporate activities: journalism, an Oxbridge college and, in *Make and Break*, a manufacturing firm doing its best at a European Trade Fair. The small dramatic pot is soon hot, and merrily boiling over: the comings and goings, misunderstandings, crossed purposes, and plenty of self-centred energy send the action shooting forwards, as the characters struggle gamely to maintain their equilibrium. The confinement of the well-made play acts as a spur for Frayn's imagination so that, by writing compact comedies about people working together, he is able to explore large issues. *Make and Break* is about using other people to achieve one's own ends, and damaging them in the process. In Michael Frayn's comedies an audience can sense the difficulty and necessity of living peacefully together, even while it laughs at the absurdities of attempts to do so.

The confinement of a well-made play has been taken by some writers several steps further, so that only a very few characters, caged and exhibited, battle for a resolution of conflicting purposes. E. A. Whitehead's *Alpha Beta* (1972), with only two characters, anatomises the morality of a marriage. Robert Holman's *German Skerries* (1977) has only four characters who meet around a hut on the sea coast in Yorkshire; here most of the action is unforced and slow-paced, but the cries of sea-birds help to alert attention to the larger issues implicit in the talk and silences. Christopher Hampton's *Treats* (1976) has a single setting in which the furnishings are changed as time passes and the trio of characters change relationships. Hampton's earlier *The Philanthropist* (1970) has more characters, but they are held together around the most witty and nervous of the bunch ('I'm a man without conviction — I think') as the play exhibits the dangers of contemporary intellectuality; it is subtitled 'a bourgeois comedy', as if to emphasise the conventional structure.

The most assured master of the well-made play is Alan Ayckbourn. He manipulates his characters through a gamut of actions and reactions with great deftness, always providing neat preparation for future surprises so that the unexpected resolutions are not merely ingenious. In the hands of Ayckbourn, coincidences, U-turns, mistakes, transformations — all managed within one set and two and a half brief hours — heighten and refine an audience's awareness, and release laughter. Recognition of the skill needed to maintain a fiction of consistent and continuous reality adds to the pleasures of the evening's entertainment.

In *Relatively Speaking*, first produced in London in 1967, the action moves from a bed-sitting room to the terrace of a house in the country, but once the play arrives there, it stays. The plot is involuted. Greg visits Philip and Sheila, thinking that he is visiting the parents of Ginny, the girl he wants to marry. But in fact Philip is Ginny's boss and, up to now, her lover; he has no daughter. Philip's wife Sheila knows nothing of all this, but seems to be sitting on her own secrets. Having got his characters into the unlikely situation, Ayckbourn does not rush them or lend them special eloquence or outrageous comic business: they move slowly, caught on the pin, and so expose their familiar defences, hesitations, small acts of courage, moments of enlightenment. The drama is kept funnily and movingly within the scale and emphasis of everyday living.

Some critics have dismissed Ayckbourn as a writer who can offer no more than 'light comedy'; but he seems always to be intent on making an audience look and listen very closely; he is so deft and makes so little fuss that one can even fear that the best laugh may pass unnoticed.

Ayckbourn has never settled into a single way of using the tried resources of the well-made play. *The Norman Conquests* (1973—4) are three interlocking plays, each one about the same people spending the same weekend in the same house; but one play shows what happens in the sitting room, another what happens in the dining room, and the third is a view of what happens in the garden. Each has a different focus and to see the plays in sequence gives a three-channel treatment of the same events.

Subject matter changes as constantly as presentation. The characters are all drawn from the middle-class, but many different events happen on and off stage, from death by drowning or a heart attack during a game of tennis, to a hilarious historical pageant or a gang of boy scouts running amok at a garden fete. *Sisterly Feelings* (1980) starts with a funeral off-stage and ends with a wedding and the opening of a new toy-shop. Moreover, Ayckbourn wrote this play in four different ways, allowing the events shown in any one performance to be determined according to luck and a moment's casual choice. Two sisters, Abigail and Dorcas, toss a coin to choose who should go off with the handsome athletic intruder, and later in the play, whoever has won the first round must make a rapid decision whether to stick with her fancy or not. Whichever way the play is performed there is a picnic, but then the choice is either a night spent under canvas or a cross-country run. The complicated series of possibilities needs a diagram in the programme to make sure that the audience understands all that might have happened. But whichever way the play is performed, the last scene is absolutely identical; and Abigail agrees with Dorcas when she says that the main thing in life is to exercise one's own choice. These words sound very hollow when an audience knows how much and, finally, how little has depended on chance and on a hurried decision. By an elaborate game with the patterns of a well-made play, Ayckbourn has represented the absurd pretension of a defiant individualism. Is life like a well-made play? Is any conclusion more than a moment's convenient pause?

Writing two and more plays a year, Ayckbourn must be one of the very few contemporary dramatists to equal Shakespeare's regular output. He seems inexhaustible: in his hands the 'old-fashioned' well-made play still lives and allows him to examine whatever it is that causes our irremovable and often ridiculous unrest.

A Sense of the Present

Postwar British dramatists are quite unlike their predecessors in that they are subsidised by the State. It is a new world. There are bursaries, royalty supplements, resident-playwright schemes, writer's workshops — all designed to encourage dramatists and to help them learn their craft when they are not able to fend for themselves. It is a thriving world, too, for never have so many plays been written; and it is quite likely that never have so many been performed. Only the Elizabethan and Jacobean theatre has rivalled ours, and on my reckoning even that golden age must have fallen several hundreds short in any one year. Much attention is given to new work: there are prizes for the year's Best Plays and the year's Most Promising Dramatist.

The State's encouragement has gone beyond the provision of funds and facilities. It has also done away with the theatrical censorship which until 28 September 1968 had been administered successively by the Royal Master of Revels and the Lord Chamberlain. Theatre is now free to respond to any aspect of life without having to satisfy a worried court official that the script to be performed contains no 'profanity or impropriety of language' and no 'offensive personalities or representations of living persons'. The vitality of new British drama in the 1960s provided the groundswell of public concern that brought about a reform that had long been sought by the theatrical profession. And since that time, the freedom from censorship has, in turn, been one of the attractions of the theatre for writers. The newest art forms of film and television are governed by a need to satisfy mass audiences and prove wide commercial viability — considerations that have brought their own, less codified and less responsible forms of censorship.

Many British dramatists of the 1970s and 1980s write about present awareness. Sometimes a story from the past is shown from the author's own perspective, as in John Mortimer's *Voyage Round My Father* (1970—71). Often the filmic device of flash-back achieves something of the same effect, for example, in the work of David Mercer, a dramatist as much at home in television as theatre. In Alan Bennett's *The Old Country* (1977), an exile confronts visitors from an earlier existence.

But the future is a more common touchstone for the present in the work of younger writers: contrasts, the natural source of power in drama, are derived at least as much from 'what can happen next?' as from 'how has this come about?'. Howard Barker, Howard Brenton, Snoo Wilson, Jonathan Gems have all set plays in the future, and still more dramatists write of the present as it wheels swiftly towards the next change of consciousness.

Barrie Keefe has written a series of plays in which the central characters are from his own East London background but of a generation younger than himself (*Gimme Shelter*, a trilogy of short plays, 1977). He was a journalist before writing for the stage and he has kept the ability to catch attention and report directly. He provides a sense of actual, unliterary and undoctored speech, sharp and lively confrontations, platforms for protestors and unexpected shifts of sympathy.

Most of Stephen Poliakoff's plays are centred on strong characters — often on one dominant character who has a clearly defined and striking function in contemporary life. The leading character of *City Sugar* (1975) is a radio disc-jockey. *American Days* (1979) is about a big business-man of the pop industry. *Summer Party* (1979) has a large cast, but Kramer, a very senior police officer, holds the centre of attention. Such characters are instantly recognisable in popular terms, but they are not stereotypes. Kramer, the policeman, behaves like a star-performer in order to keep the peace. The play is concerned with an open-air pop-concert and, when everything goes wrong, Kramer actually takes command on-stage, addressing the huge and by this time dissatisfied audience as if he were the star of the evening. He keeps his cool in a moment of high tension and Stephen Poliakoff dwells on that moment. The structure of the play ensures that the audience gets to know Kramer slowly, step by step as other people encounter and challenge him.

Stephen Poliakoff says he is not a 'political writer', making statements about what should be done to improve the world, but one who looks at the world around him, aware of ideas that are in the air. His job is to create characters belonging to that world and set them in action so that they hold and move an audience.

In a time when theatre can feel threatened by the instantly available entertainment of TV, film and video, these plays take on all that part of our lives. They are about powerful people, the pop industry, political propaganda, gambling, big business and urban deprivation. But they place the audience at the centre of the action, in a way that the two dimensional image of a screen can never do. They are written with imaginative energy and cunning so that individual 'star' characters are projected towards crises that audiences are led to share.

More and more authors are drawn to the theatre — by the 1980s the major subsidised companies in Britain were being sent thousands of new scripts each year — but the difficulties of writing a good play seem to grow at a similar rate. While drama may well be the form most suitable for expressing the complexity of modern living

40

and modern consciousness, infinite care and considerable risks must be taken if it is to do so. Fortunately there is an unforced, unstoppable ferment in British theatre today that gives hope that each new play to reach production may be a true adventure or — just possibly — a masterpiece.

Part Two

Twenty-Five Plays

The Workhouse Donkey

John Arden says that when he thinks of 'the Drama' a popular nineteenth-century engraving of an actor in character, with fixed histrionic attitude and 'features contorted with apparently immobile passion', comes inevitably into his mind: 'its crude primary colours and its tinsel embellishments' present the figments of his imagination.

This is the style of *The Workhouse Donkey*, subtitled 'A Vulgar Melodrama'. As Albert Hunt says, 'the one level the play can't work on is that of straight naturalism'; it affirms 'that human behaviour *can* be richly and grotesquely and joyfully implausible', and so it demands 'an equally bold and outrageous form of theatre.'

In a preface Arden writes of the difficulties he experienced in containing his 'labyrinthine and intractable' material within the bounds of conventional theatre and a report of the first performance by Charles Marowitz echoes this: he thought the play should be either compressed still further or 'expanded into a true, rambling Jonsonian comedy'.

The basis of action is simple: a new Chief Constable, Colonel Feng, arrives in a Yorkshire town where the Socialist party has been in power for thirty uninterrupted years; as a non-party man, he seeks to expose and punish corruption, but he fails; he leaves the place much as he found it, except that Tories and Socialists are sharing the same platform to reopen a strip-club as an Art Gallery.

The Socialist Mayor and the Conservative leader, with their wives and supporters, a publican with his customers, policemen, journalists, dancers, hostesses, lovers and demonstrators — a cross-section of the town — are projected into

45

such bold, animated and often funny life that the play has been compared with Ben Jonson's *Bartholomew Fair* (1614) and the *Wasps* and *Frogs* of Aristophanes (*c*. 448– *c*. 380 BC). The main characters often address the audience directly to specify their attitudes, advance the plot, or make a joke. Prose is abandoned sometimes for verse, so that the drama changes gear for more complex character-involvement or more buoyant forward drive. When Butter-thwaite rebels against conformity and robs the town-hall safe of £500 to pay his gambling debts, a crowd of journalists take flashlight photographs of eight specified confrontations. Music, song and dance, in imitation of various popular idioms, build up entries and exits, and hold dramatic climaxes.

In the last scene, anarchy triumphs. Butterthwaite breaks into a dignified public occasion, supported by drunken and fighting 'layabouts', with placards reading 'All fine art is a hearty fart', 'You can't gild a mucky lily', and so on. Isolated from his rabble, he denounces both friends and enemies in words borrowed from Jehovah of the Old Testament. As he is arrested and removed from the stage, he sings of himself as the poor old Donkey — irrational, dirty and beastlike. It only remains for Feng to leave, promising to whitewash the police activities, and for the others to unite in affirming their intention to keep the whole town clean.

Arden confesses to the formlessness of his play, but that was probably a game he played with the critics. In fact, the plan of *The Workhouse Donkey* is arranged carefully and schematically to celebrate irrationality. Many of its characters are politically polarized, but not so that political issues can be established fully or pursued; above all, the play presents Arden's estimation of the vulgar attributes of the 'Donkey'.

See also pp. 17–19.

ALAN AYCKBOURN   **Bedroom Farce**

b. 1939   *Scarborough, 1975; London, 1977*

Alan Ayckbourn, according to Michael Billington, is
'at his most serious when he is at his funniest'. The very
title of *Bedroom Farce* marks it as a test case, and as
soon as the curtain rises on a triple set, showing three
separate bedrooms, multiple possibilities for laughter
are in view.

Separately, the couples inhabiting each room are managing life together with some assurance. Nick, a hyperactive
young executive, is lying in his trendy bed with a dislocated
back, and Jan his bright young wife makes sure he is as
'comfy' as may be. Malcolm and Kate are getting ready for
their house-warming party in a half-decorated, under-
furnished bedroom. Ernest and Delia prepare to go out for
dinner on their wedding anniversary, tolerating each other's
foibles in the large bedroom of a Victorian family house in
which they now live alone. But the cast includes one
further couple, Susannah and Trevor, whose bedroom is
not shown and whose marriage is in danger of break-down.
They go to the house-warming separately and their insecurities and impulsive actions precipitate frustration,
anger, pain and extreme egotism in each of the other characters. Further circumstances heighten the drama and absurdity as the action switches from one bedroom to another,
and sometimes continues in all three simultaneously: at an
earlier time Jan had been on the point of marrying Trevor;
the quality, service and cost of the celebratory dinner have
proved to be appalling; and Susannah arrives in the early
hours for advice from Delia, her mother-in-law. Each
character is caught off-balance and wobbles helplessly on
the verge of a precipice.

47

The gigantic improbabilities and sexual outrageousness that are natural to farce are not the basis of this comedy. In the programme for the London première, Ayckbourn explained: 'Comedy, I read somewhere, consists of larger than life characters in real situations. Farce, on the other hand, portrays real characters projected into incredible situations. *Bedroom Farce* is a comedy about real characters who, projected into incredible situations, start behaving in a larger than life manner as the situations appear to them too horribly real.'

Through the laughter, deep feelings are exposed, but they are not often expressed directly in words. Nick is the most articulate, but his true consciousness is sensed as much in ill-tempered cries of pain and silent physical exertions as in devastating descriptions of other people's shortcomings. Trevor is able to say that his own reflection in a glass appalls him and that he cannot find three good reasons why he should not commit suicide, but his thoughts outpace anything he says and words peter out into silence. Susannah says a great deal about herself and seems to thrive in doing so, but her deepest resource, is to get alone and tell herself, out loud and repeatedly, and in the simplest words, that she *is* attractive. Ernest seeks reassurance by reading aloud from *Tom Brown's Schooldays* and gains some approval from Delia by providing pilchards on toast to eat in bed. Malcolm struggles unavailingly with a make-it-yourself kit of a dressing-table for his wife.

No one gets much sleep in the play, but when the Saturday night turns into very early Sunday morning, Trevor and Susannah have come together in someone else's bed; he cuddles up and falls asleep and she, holding her husband's head in her arms, tells herself that people still find her attractive.

See also pp. 35–7.

HOWARD BARKER

No End of Blame:
scenes of overcoming

b. 1946

Oxford and London, 1981

During the interval of one of his plays a member of the
audience approached Howard Barker and said: 'You're the
author, aren't you? I'd like to protest that I don't really
know what this play's about.' 'But it's only the interval,'
came the reply, 'How can you expect to know what the
play's about at the interval?'

No End of Blame is designed to keep an audience guess-
ing. It starts in 1918 in the Carpathian Mountains, where a
naked woman with an expression of terror on her face
stands centre-stage while a battle-weary Hungarian soldier
sits with a rifle at his side making a pencil sketch of her
figure. Soon another soldier enters, approaches the woman,
and begins to strip himself naked. The men fight; the
woman runs away; an artillery bombardment is heard
from off-stage and then other soldiers enter and an execution is ordered. But the naked man's life is spared while
he improvises a rhyming poem. All this occupies no
more than five or ten minutes, and before this scene is
complete — the first of a total of twelve — a war is won,
Communist soldiers take control, and the naked man, Bela
Veracek, saves the life of the officer who had ordered his
own death.

Subsequently Bela travels to the USSR and becomes a
famous cartoonist; he then reaches Britain where he is again
successful and controlled by new and different masters. At
the age of seventy-five he tries to commit suicide but he is
put in hospital, together with Grigor, the soldier who had
been sketching at the beginning of the play. The play ends
as Bela calls for a pencil so that he can work on a cartoon

that will 'assign the blame' for the overwhelming madness and pain that he experiences in the world. The basic visual image of each scene is strong, and the forty-one characters — who can be performed by one dozen actors — bring a wide range of contrasted reactions to each developing crisis.

The play argues about the role of an artist in society, the relative importance of timeless beauty and timely truth, art *versus* cartoon, personal vision *versus* public utility, perfected literature *versus* an effective use of language in real situations. But it is not an argumentative play which culminates in a full and eloquent statement or centres on a formal trial or sustained debate between mighty opposites. Its characteristic speech is deliberate, but spare, sharp, idiomatic, short-phrased. Meaning is enforced by hard and precise imagery, repetition, lithe humour and fierce spurts of utterance marked by a frequent use of capitals in the printed text. Surprise and new invention catch attention after any temporary resolution: a flower-bed is despoiled; a tea-lady interrupts an investigative committee to serve tea. Bela and Grigor are held up to view, time and again, until the grounds for their actions are revealed, choked out in words, with a sense of indignation, wounding humour or resolution; then the story moves away again to further engagement and new pillories.

No End of Blame is an insistent, ambitious play, a series of parables, each given the speed, clarity, punch and timeliness of a cartoon, and the whole carefully articulated to demonstrate the grounds of responsible action in a politically repressive world. It provides bracing entertainment.

See also p. 23.

Born near Dublin, educated at Trinity College Dublin and settling in Paris in the 1930s, Beckett has written most of his plays in French, subsequently translating them himself into English. But no guide to British drama since the Second World War would be complete without an account of his work. He has always made severe demands upon actors and audiences, but every year since the first London production of *Waiting for Godot* in 1955 his plays have been performed in Britain. Of that first première Harold Hobson wrote that 'It is bewildering. It is exasperating. It is insidious. It is exciting. . . . Something that will securely lodge in a corner of your mind for as long as you live.'

Beckett's plays present specific and inescapable symbols of man's conscious life. Each has a strong central image, physically represented on the stage: two tramps and a tree (*Godot*), three heads in urns (*Play*), two parents in dustbins (*Endgame*), a mouth speaking in darkness (*Not I*). An audience is not told what these symbols mean: but performance gives them life within their minds.

Happy Days is the one major play written first in English. Winnie, its heroine, is embedded to above her waist in a low mound, covered with scorched grass; the light is blazing, and at her back a painted cloth represents an unbroken plain and the sky. She is woken from sleep by a piercing bell that rings twice before she opens her eyes and welcomes 'Another heavenly day'. Winnie is an optimist and works hard to keep herself in good spirits: she examines the contents of a large bag lying beside her on the mound; she attends to her face and appearance; she tells a story and recalls incidents and quotations from the past. In the

51

second Act, there is far less that she can do because she is now buried up to her neck. Behind the mound is Willie, her husband. When he comes into view he amuses himself with a newspaper and a 'filthy' postcard. Winnie and he exchange a few words — just to know that he is within earshot is a comfort to her — and in the play's last moments he comes round to the front of the mound, *dressed to kill*. A Browning revolver taken from the bag in Act One lies between them, and the audience does not know whether Willie wishes to kill Winnie or to kiss her. All he can whisper is 'Win'; and then she sings a short love-song from *The Merry Widow* and smiles briefly. The play ends with the two of them looking at each other, unsmilingly, and a long pause.

Happy Days uses only two actors and a carefully-chosen minimum of stage effects, but it is powerful in performance. Beckett wrote in his study of *Proust* (1931) that 'the work of art is neither created nor chosen, but discovered, uncovered, excavated, pre-existing with the artist, a law of his nature.' This play represents his view of existence in extreme isolation or at the end of civilization. (In an early draft its action occurred, specifically, after a nuclear device had been exploded.) It is also a funny play — an early subtitle was '*A Low Comedy*' — because it shows how pretension, inconsequence and ignorance are at work in this struggle for life.

The source of power in *Happy Days* does not lie in Winnie's optimism that blinds her to the truth of her situation, but in what Peter Brook has called the 'few rare flashes' in which she glimpses her true situation. Because of these and the eloquent shape of the drama as a whole, an audience leaves this black play, as Brook says, 'nourished and enriched, with a lighter heart, full of a strange irrational joy. Poetry, nobility, beauty, magic — suddenly these suspect words are back in the theatre once more.'

See also pp. 9—11.

ROBERT BOLT
b. 1924

A Man for All Seasons

London, 1960

Before turning to the theatre Robert Bolt wrote a dozen radio plays and had worked for years as a school master. Then, after success in the theatre, he went on to write many film scripts, some of them large in scale like *Lawrence of Arabia* and *Doctor Zhivago*.

His first play, *Flowering Cherry*, had been conventional in form (see p. 3), but *A Man for All Seasons* is much closer to a radio documentary narrative, telling the story of Sir Thomas More's opposition to King Henry VIII's divorce from his first wife, Catherine of Aragon, a matter of politics and conscience which led him to resign the Lord Chancellorship of England and then to accept his own execution for high treason.

The story is presented to the audience by a character called 'The Common Man' who gives relevant facts and dates with breezy good humour, sometimes reading from papers that descend on stage and into his hands — and, on occasion, taking the story years into the future — and sometimes speaking for himself as he assumes the roles of steward, boatman, Foreman of the Jury and, lastly, executioner. This device gives an air of charade to the play's development, but this is offset by Bolt's more subtle skill in demonstrating the political and moral issues in domestic terms: Sir Thomas is seen with Alice, his outspoken, straightforward wife, with Margaret, his scholarly daughter, William Roper, an earnest, easily convinced young man who becomes his son-in-law, as well as with the young King, Cardinal Wolsey, Cromwell, Cranmer and other men at the centre of power and intrigue. Besides more obviously weighty matters, a sumptuous supper is prepared for a royal guest who leaves it untasted; the King blows his whistle as if still in charge of the *Royal Harry*, a ship he has just launched; wine is drunk; music is played.

And at the centre of all is Sir Thomas More, a man of intellectual clarity, subtlety and strength, and of generous and warm feeling. Paul Scofield created this role on stage and film, and, both in the seeming spontaneity of Bolt's invention of his personal life and in the measured, dignified and courageous words taken from the original accounts of More's own statements at his trial, demonstrated the theatre's ability to bring a character from the past alive so that a modern audience can engage in the crises of his life with immediacy and keen feeling. As John Russell Taylor said 'Bolt offers substantial acting parts for substantial actors . . . and well-made, reliable entertainment for intelligent people.'

EDWARD BOND

b. 1934

Bingo: scenes of money and death
Exeter, 1973; London, 1974

The beginning is idyllic, as Shakespeare strolls into his garden in Stratford on an autumn afternoon, carrying a sheet of paper; he sits and reads. But then surprises begin. The poet says almost nothing until the entry of Combe, a local landowner and businessman. The audience realises then that the paper is not a poem or a speech from a play, but a document drawn up to safeguard Shakespeare's income when Combe encloses some common land for sheep-grazing and so deprives numerous poor farmers of their livelihoods.

Bingo is a short play of six scenes in which Shakespeare is shown living among poor, hungry and oppressed people, half of them nameless, who suffer, struggle and die. His wife and daughter are frustrated and bitter. Bond has not attempted a strict historical reconstruction. He has given Shakespeare only one daughter, Judith, and has invented an old woman who is able to offer him some comfort. This woman has a husband with the mind of a child because he was hit with the blunt side of an axe when a fellow conscript was killing an enemy. Bond follows tradition in having Shakespeare die in 1616 after going out for a drink with Ben Jonson; but the details of this are altered, in that the burning of the Globe has been moved three years later so that his fellow dramatist has been sent by the players to ask for a new play to open the rebuilt theatre. Moreover, Shakespeare does not die from a cold caught on the way home; we do see him out on the heath at night wandering about on the land that is being enclosed, but he returns home to kill himself by poison.

The drinking-scene starts the second part of the play and is by far the liveliest of the six. Jonson is an active man, crafty, practical, suspicious and, as he confesses, fired by hatred. He praises Shakespeare for his 'serenity' — and this echoes the praise of many twentieth-century moralizing critics — but the word cuts more deeply than Jonson is aware. Shakespeare has come to realise that he has spent the latter part of his life cultivating his own peace of mind at the cost of isolating himself from other men and women; his art has become a refuge or retreat.

The issues of the play are presented in stark contrasts that alert and inform the audience's attention. At the end of the first half a beggar-girl hangs dead on a gibbet, her face twisted with pain and her filthy body covered with a sack. Close by, the poor eat and talk together, saying that by rights she should have been burnt. On a bench

Shakespeare sits facing away from the body, silent. When two of the young men who are protesting actively against the enclosures start to pray aloud, secure in their moral judgement, Shakespeare walks slowly away, his face expressing nothing. When Judith comes and calls for him, he returns and, for the first time in the play, speaks at length. He is stupified at the suffering of 'unaccommodated man' and knows that in a world which is set on the pursuit and maintenance of possessions no one will ever listen to what he can say about it. In silence he can find no higher wisdom. The old woman offers to take him home, speaking of her own troubles. He listens quietly and then speaks again: while the girl was being hanged on the previous day, he had gone to the quiet river and a swan had flown by him up-stream; he had heard its breath, sighing, and he could hear its wings long after it had disappeared. He imagines the swan now, as if it were a woman in a white dress running along an empty street. Then he thinks again, mostly in silence, of the girl's death; he goes to the gibbet and says, very simply, that she is still both perfect and beautiful.

The play is both intensely felt and clearly conceived — to an extent that infuriated some critics at its first performance. Each scene moves deliberately, marking the issues carefully and precisely, but, as Tony Coult says, this is also a 'very personal play' and passionate convictions inform the entire work. Shakespeare is presented as a 'corrupt seer' in a 'barbarous civilisation', like an author in the late twentieth-century.

See also pp. 19–22.

HOWARD BRENTON

b. 1942

Epsom Downs

London, 1977

The purpose of *Epsom Downs* can be stated simply: to re-present Derby Day of 1977, the year of Queen Elizabeth II's Silver Jubilee, when Lestor Piggott won on The Minstrel at five to one. For a painter, photographer or film-maker this project would be straightforward, but for a dramatist it sets complicated problems. A whole world has to be put on stage, an excited cross-section of British society working and enjoying itself, a day full of unusual encounters, a chance to win or lose a fortune, and the race itself. More-over Brenton had to achieve all this for Joint Stock, a small touring theatre company, who could field only nine actors. The result is, as Irving Wardle says, 'a teeming Brueghel-like composition . . . a marvel of expressive economy'.

About a hundred characters are brought on stage, from a three-year-old child, stable boys, bookmakers and a book-maker's wife, buskers, drunks, a bunny girl, lovers and vendors, to the opposite end of the social spectrum with horse-owners, society men and women, the Aga Khan with his body-guard and, just off-stage, the Queen being driven round the course. From early in the morning the crowd gathers together, and anticipation mounts until the race is won; and then follows dispersal and tidying-up.

Only extreme concentration of means prevents confusion and distortion. Speeches have been considered carefully so that they both carry an immediate message and imply a continuing involvement in the common event and social reality. This is no documentary drama, presenting slices of actual life, but an economical use of time and words so that each mind is truly present and active, each figure a

57

human presence. The stage-picture often changes, and changes rapidly, but every moment has density and depth.

Interlocking sub-plots, each related to the running of the Derby, add to the impression of abundant life. They also ensure that some characters have greater prominence: the story of Jocks, a stable-boy who gets the sack, leads to the moment when he is given a £10 note and a kiss by a gipsy girl; Lord Rack blunders vigorously through the play until he asserts that 'even an old atheist, socialist life-peer has to say — God's in his heaven and all's right with the world', and then falls to the ground; the evangelists, Mr Tillotson and Miss Motrom, stop preaching about hell-fire and revert to betting and drink; Sandy risks his life-savings, and his wife, Margaret, holds on to an idea of a free and good life.

The excitement of the race-meeting is expressed with the greatest economy of all, boldly and physically. Horses are naked, bridled actors, a jockey is an actor who walks on his knees. The race itself is one actor festooned with regalia who makes a lively display, verbally and physically, of all the events, changes of tempo and uncertainties; he is followed on and off stage by a crowd of all the other actors.

A few characters have other origins: the ghost of Emily Davison, who had thrown herself in front of the King's horse in the Derby of 1913, and the lunatics from a neighbouring asylum who are allowed out, as a treat, to clear up the rubbish left by the Derby crowd. By these means further perspectives are suggested. The play does not end with a unifying, comic resolution in the manner of a Jacobean comedy (Joint Stock had recently staged Barrie Keefe's re-working of Middleton's *A Mad World My Masters*): Derby Day is shown as a special event in an unsettled and disoriented world.

See also pp. 7—8 and 23—4.

A Taste of Honey

London, 1958

At one level *A Taste of Honey* is an unremarkable play: it tells a short, affecting story about a small family. But it centres on Josephine (or Jo), a girl still younger than the dramatist who was only seventeen when she started writing it and eighteen when it became an instant success in London. Besides, as Kenneth Tynan points out, it 'deals joyfully with what might, in other hands, have been a tragic situation.'

Jo's mother, Helen, is a 'semi-whore' and goes off to live with Peter, a 'brash car-salesman'; Jo becomes pregnant by a young black sailor whom she can hardly expect to see again, although she wears his Woolworth's ring on a ribbon round her neck and thinks of him as a handsome African prince who sings marvellously. When he has left, Jo is comforted by Geof, a retiring, gay art-student, who moves in after meeting her at a fair and starts making preparations for the baby's birth. Helen, however, falls out with Peter and returns just in time to take over the role of grandmother-to-be: Geof leaves, having placed a note by a Teddy-bear, saying 'I love you'.

The vitality of the play comes from its unaffected, north-country dialogue — 'I write as people speak', said the author — and still more from the portrayal of Jo. She is clear-eyed and quick-witted, affectionate and imaginative by nature but wary and cynical from experience. All her contradictions are unaffectedly apparent: she wants to love and be loved, and yet she also wants to be independent; she can lie, both to herself and others, and she is also transparently honest.

The published text of 1959 is the copyright of Joan

Littlewood's Theatre Workshop (see pp. 25—6) and incorporates changes made in rehearsal. These involved the final resolution (Jo originally left for hospital and Geof was on stage as the curtain fell), a general tightening-up of dialogue and action and, most significantly, the addition of a number of lines addressed to the audience and directions for music from a jazz trio who played dance tunes to bring characters on and off stage, supported some of the singing and closed Act One with 'Here Comes The Bride' for Helen's departure. Joan Littlewood's production was in what John Russell Taylor calls 'a sort of magnified realism, in which everything is like life but somehow larger than life'. When Jo went off-stage, Avis Bunnage, as Helen, would turn to the audience to gripe, taunt, comment on or mock her daughter. Short asides in the printed text may owe more to Joan Littlewood's desire to enliven the performances than to the author's sense of what could actually be spoken.

Considerable variety of tone and style is found within the small dimensions of this play: nursery-rhymes, games and music-hall jokes, together with everyday routines, blazing rows and reconciliations; simple but effectively placed repetitions; and silences. Geof castigates women for selfishness and masochism; Helen and Jo deliver 'home truths' whenever they see the opportunity. And at the centre is a longing for peace, security, dignity and even power. On one of the rare occasions when the young author risked a literary note, Jo says 'We are all princes in our own little kingdom'.

MICHAEL FRAYN   Donkey's Years

b. 1933   *London, 1976*

The heroes of Michael Frayn's early novels and the main
characters of his stage comedies written from 1970 onwards
all struggle against overwhelming pressures in the world
around them. *Donkey's Years* set in 'one of the lesser
colleges, at one of the older universities' brings half a dozen
men back for a reunion, twenty years after graduation.
They are shown on arrival, after a long evening's drinking
and at breakfast-time the next day. With varying degrees
of earnestness they affirm that they have not changed at
all, but also that they *have* changed. Some remember
decisive moments but have little sense of how they became
decisive. All of them are more or less helpless while the
years carry them onwards, certain only that they are be-
coming older and before long will be old.

To these fools of time are added a young Research
Fellow, the Head Porter and Lady Driver, wife of the
Master of the College, who is absent in Montreal. With
them come many complications, especially the industrial
action which sends the Porter off duty at midnight and the
active curiosity of the 'College Mistress' concerning Roddy
Moore who is on the list of guests and whom she had
abandoned years ago for the security and success of
her present husband.

Once these characters have been established in Act I, the
action moves boisterously and preposterously forward in
Acts II and III. Clothes are exchanged, speeches get mis-
understood, bedroom doors are closed rapidly, furniture
collapses, Roddy never turns up and Snell, a depressed
research scientist whom no one remembers, is given his
set of rooms. Lady Driver is locked out of the Master's

61

Lodging and spends much of the third Act concealing herself, first behind a door that has to be kept open (which sometimes happens by accident, sometimes by intent) and then behind a newspaper held over her head — she is by now either wearing men's clothing or else a bed-sheet. The usual anarchies of farce are sustained by the strenuous efforts of the guests, whose befuddled memories tell them that the anarchy of youth — its casual freedoms, absurdities and improprieties — had perhaps held the secret of their education, happiness and former selves. Desperate pursuit of a second chance keeps the action overflowing and the jokes multiplying.

The characters are very clearly delineated and — this is part of the essence of the comedy — unchanging. C.D.P.B. Headingly, MA, MP, a junior Minister, is a successful public man, competent at everything, but alarmed at any possibility of publicity. D.J. Buckle, MB, MRCS, is a surgeon who is ponderous, loyal, independent and, at times, impressively decisive. Alan Quine, BA, is a civil servant, conservative in appearance, sardonic in manner and expert at making others feel ill at ease. R.D. Sainsbury, MA, is a 'ghastly, camp little man' in a clerical collar. N.O.P. Tate, MA, is a 'comfortable, cosy man, with a womanly manner and a little moustache', who has become a very popular writer. Snell, the outsider, is unimpressive except when alone and then he reveals a fierce, unbridled and narrow determination.

Rosemary, Lady Driver, presides over the whole play. This is not because she achieves very much beyond keeping her head reasonably cool. But she is sharper and more resourceful than any of the men and in Act II she has a long emotional speech about her life and memories which is intended for Roddy Moore but, owing to extreme shortsightedness, is delivered in full measure to a silent Snell. When she sees Snell at last, her triumph is that she closes her eyes for some moments and then continues to take command of herself — and of others if need be and opportunity offers — right on to the end of the play.

See also p. 34.

SIMON GRAY	Otherwise Engaged
b. 1936	*London, 1975*

Simon, the hero of Simon Gray's *Otherwise Engaged*, has the same objective at the end of the play as at the beginning — to sit down in the living-room of his own house to listen to a new and complete recording of Wagner's last, compassionate and visionary opera, *Parsifal*. When this is achieved, the music swells, lights fade and the curtain falls. Simon has been on stage throughout as the other characters come and go, reporting various personal successes and disasters, and all making demands on his time and attention.

In form, the play could hardly be more simple. Interest lies in its exposure of the central character and the impression it gives of the people and events around him. John Barber says that it is 'a brilliantly funny and penetrating study' of modern intellectual consciousness.

Simon is a successful publisher, but it seems that he has written the blurb for a book he has not read. He has been married for some years and both partners have agreed to have no children, but he is pestered and exploited by Dave, a young student to whom he has let the unwanted rooms of his house, and he learns that Beth, his wife, is pregnant with a child that may not be his. He attempts

63

civil conversation with everyone who enters his living-
room, but this does not prevent him from making wounding remarks, not least to Wood, whom he had known in
his schooldays and who is now, as then, pitiable and
undistinguished. Although Simon has the tone of un-
assuming assurance and a keen sense of other people's
needs, his repeated efforts at peace-making have only
contrary effects. He is often wounded himself or forced to
pay for small achievements. He feels something like envy
for Wood's hopeless devotion to a young girl who is
indifferent and even cruel to him. When at last he is
able to listen to *Parsival*, he has to sit with Jeff, a restless
and cynical critic for whom he has little or no regard.
Simon can lose himself in the deeply symbolic music only
after hearing that his lodger is bringing two more people to
live in his house and listening on the ansaphone to Wood's
detailed and gloating account of his own suicide; and Jeff
has accused him of tipping-off the police who have just
caught him for driving when drunk.

During most of the play, the dialogue alternates between
a sharp-edged conversational ease and unease, but at times
it has the sustained eloquence of a more classical drama:
Jeff demolishes foreigners and homosexuals in a bloody-
minded threnody for England; Simon denounces Dave for
taking politeness at face value; Beth castigates Simon as a
freak who cares too much for too little. At such moments
the audience is held by the power and conviction of speech
but also senses the deceptiveness of intellectual confidence. Both appeasement and aggression fail in their
purposes; only the author's passion for articulate clarity
is constant throughout this closely observed and well
managed play.

See pp. 33—4.

Comedians

Nottingham and London, 1975

Eddie Waters, a retired stand-up comic, has been teaching his art to six students in evening-classes in Manchester. Act I of *Comedians* shows them getting ready for their final assessment by Bert Challoner, an agent working from London. In Act II, they perform their chosen acts in a working-man's club before an audience waiting to get back to Bingo. In Act III, they listen to Challoner's judgements.

Trevor Griffiths has used the public contest to contrast different attitudes towards performance and life, as represented by the contestants. He has also contrasted the two professionals. Eddie explains that what matters is not a comedian's jokes but what lies behind them, his ability to see what his audience shies away from: a true joke is not a stereotype, but a fresh experience that liberates both will and desire. Challoner, on the other hand, says that a good comic leads his audience by the nose in the direction it wants to go, which is towards escape: he need not like his audience, but he has got to make them love him.

After the contest, only two students are offered work because only they have followed Challoner's prescriptions. An Irish student has stayed earnestly on the single topic of being an Irishman in England. The performers of a double-act have become terrified after one of them tried to improvise. The total failure is Eddie's most gifted student, Gethin Price.

Price has used entirely new material. His face is slightly whitened like a clown's, but he wears the clothes of a young supporter of Manchester United Football Club. After an abortive attempt to play a small violin, he crushes the instrument beneath his foot, like a spent cigarette; and he says — to himself, not to the audience — that he would like to smash up a train. Then a dummy cut-out of an affluent, middle-class couple in evening dress appears behind him and he proceeds to taunt, mock and insult it. His hatred is expressed deliberately, brutally and incisively. The act is completely unfunny, right to its end in assertive chants of a football crowd and four bars of 'The Red Flag' played on a new violin.

Eddie and Price are then left alone. The ex-'Lancashire Lad' tells how a post-war visit to the museum at Buchenwald Concentration Camp had killed the next Jewish joke he had heard; for him, no jokes were left. This was not because he loved Jews or hated Nazis, but because he knew that he had experienced an instinctive pleasure as he looked at the relics of appalling atrocities. Eddie acknowledges the brilliance of Price's act, but accuses him of being motivated by hatred and not truth. To this Price retorts that truth has to hit like a fist: because people are not in fact free to belong to themselves, truth is always ugly, not beautiful or entertaining. The parting of teacher and student is presented quietly: Eddie will start a new class; Price goes back to driving a van for British Rail and holding himself in readiness for the revolution that he believes must come in order to change the situation, and liberate will and desire.

Parts of *Comedians* are very funny, and the writing is exhilarating on account of its economy, accuracy and invention. But its action is planned so that the dialectical points are established inescapably in the author's own particular and passionately held terms: the effect of this is unnerving, even to members of an audience who share the opinions of the author.

See also p. 23.

Treats

London, 1976

Actors must not labour the implicit meanings of Christopher Hampton's dialogue; they should speak and behave with the apparent confidence and controlled emphasis of high comedy. Performed in this way, *Treats* will move forward with airborne ease — Ronald Hayman calls it a 'conventional' play — but it will also suggest a slow-moving drama underneath the words.

Three characters and one set — the living room of a flat in central London — are its principal elements. Ann is in possession, accompanied at first by Patrick who works in the same office. They are visited by Dave, a journalist who has just returned from three weeks in Nicosia to find himself displaced and locked out. Subsequently Ann sends Patrick away and Dave is installed once more.

The combatants in this triangle are intelligent and Hampton has contrasted them intelligently. Dave's usual ploys are both playful and destructive, his talk hard-hitting and fluent. Patrick's responses are habitually amicable and unassertive, his talk wary and carefully limited. Both men oppress the woman, who for most of the play is self-assertively still and silent.

Music from specified popular recordings concludes the first seven of nine scenes, and so provides a generally recognisable setting for the individual's drama. The two men, on separate occasions, also listen to music through earphones — the Beatles for Dave, and Bruchner for Patrick — and gain obvious pleasure from the sounds that only they hear. Occasionally references to political events or off-stage sounds are used to suggest a second, more palpable framework for the interplay of character: pro-IRA demonstrators shouting 'Send them back!' and 'Murderer!', and, when Patrick tries to re-enter the flat, the frenzied barking of Dave's dog, Arthur. So, while the drama maintains domestic proportions, the audience becomes aware of wider resonances.

On other occasions the interior drama is presented with inescapable emphasis and the closest focus. Three short scenes present only one character. In the first, Dave makes three telephone calls in different but not very convincing *personae*, and then examines himself in a mirror before playing a Bob Dylan song; he listens to it, putting it on again and then goes back in silence to the mirror. In the second, Patrick tries to get himself in good order for a day's work while the radio news is switched-on; he pays brief attention to this only when it happens to mention a particularly appalling item. He, too, looks in a mirror, but only once; and he contemplates the room before leaving, without his umbrella. Ann's solo-scene is the penultimate of the play and, like Patrick's, totally without words. She sits still for some time and then rises to turn on the TV; her chair swivels so that she watches with her back to the audience. Then she half-turns away and is seen to be weeping. After a long time, her tears turn to sobs which are seemingly uncontrollable — until she gets up suddenly and starts to make the phone call which will ask Dave to return.

These solo-scenes prepare for the silent ending, following Patrick's final departure. When Ann goes after him, Dave looks terrified; when she returns and smiles at him, he looks away; when she comes closer, he looks at her and remains, to all appearances, stone-cold. The brilliant comedy comes to a last stand which offers little in expectation for the individuals concerned besides some isolated and isolating little treats — despite the intimations of distant violence and rebellion.

See also pp. 34–5.

DAVID HARE   Teeth 'n' Smiles
b. 1947   *London, 1975*

David Hare dates the action of his play very precisely during
the night of 9 June 1969, six years and three months before
its first performance. He wants to catch an exact moment
in the history of pop music and to give an exact 'feel' of
living in England.

A rock band plays a gig at the May Ball of Jesus College,
Cambridge, and its members, together with songwriter,
roadie, p.r., manager and Maggie, their lead singer, are the
play's main characters. The first Act takes place in a college
room, the second on the lawn behind the band's stage; in
both a truck brings the equipment down front for musical
numbers.

The event is a disaster. It starts late because a plug is not
connected. Maggie gets desperately drunk and, in the second
of three sets, insults her audience. She is fired by the
manager. Drugs are found by the police. Maggie sets fire to
the marquee and goes off to prison, while the others make
off as best they can.

David Hare has chosen his characters so that the play is
an image of a wider world. Until he meets Maggie singing
ballads in the Red Lion, Arthur, the songwriter, had been
an undergraduate studying music in this very college; he is
still a romantic intellectual, seeking significance and despis-
ing almost everything. Anson is a short and stumbling
undergraduate who tries to interview Maggie and make
some sort of impression: he is studying medicine — he
keeps a human finger in his pocket and brings it out as a
conversational ploy — but he is determined to opt out of
his chosen profession and join a band in any menial
capacity. Randolph who is in attendance on Saraffian,

69

the manager, is thirty-five years old, but wears so much make-up that no-one can guess his age; he is introduced as a 'lad' who is to become a star and he appears to have no mind of his own.

In contrast, Maggie trades on her personal pain, the tragedy of her life as she usually calls it. Huge quantities of drink keep her going and only by fierce concentration does she drag music out in confrontation with an audience. She leaves for jail insisting that nobody is to feel guilty; anyone who loves her is to keep on the move.

At the end of the play, when there's no money and no girls, the characters share a need to go on. Then, during a blackout, short messages are flashed on a screen in big letters: it is 1973, and while one of the band is dead — he inhaled his own vomit — the rest are alive and well, and living in England. Then comes one more song, Maggie's song about giving the last orders aboard the Titanic.

As C. W. E. Bigsby says, David Hare's England is 'a country in which private despair is the constant. There are no models of an alternative system, no calls for working-class solidarity, only a clear-eyed analysis of moral entropy, the failure of public myths and private values.'

Teeth 'n' Smiles is both bleak and romantic, a bitter moral tale about decadence which is also a vindication of the pursuit of meaning. It vibrates with rock music and also with teeming, tight-reined rhetoric. It is a conceited comedy which is also violent and restless, a drama which an audience can recognise, in its author's words, 'as a situation in which they have been'.

See also pp. 22–3.

ANN JELLICOE   The Sport of My Mad Mother

b. 1927   *London, 1958*

This is not an easy play to read. As John Russell Taylor says, its text is a 'blueprint for production' and not a literary artefact: 'quite a lot of the dialogue, in fact, is merely "sound" — cries and ejaculations, repeated monosyllables shorn of any associative effect and used entirely for their tonal qualities.' Its validity is in performance: 'in the theatre it surges over and around one, a strange, disturbing pattern of sights and sounds that produces a corresponding series of emotional reactions from which gradually a total picture of a violent, instinctive way of life emerges.'

Introducing the play as winner of a joint third prize in *The Observer*'s new play competition, Kenneth Tynan wrote that *The Sport of My Mad Mother* 'stands in the same relationship to conventional play-making as jazz does to conventional music: in an ideal production it would have the effect of spontaneous improvisation, or of a vocal *danse macabre* that makes up its own rules and language as it goes along'. Ann Jellicoe has encouraged such a view by placing Steve, one of the characters, at one side of the stage with a drum-set and other percussive instruments and inviting him to accompany the play's action as he finds fit.

But words and music are only part of a sequence of actions: individual turns, group activities and some traces of a plot involving a group of teenagers who ride high on their fantasies. Greta, an Australian, is the Mad Mother, who also acts on one occasion like a repressive schoolmistress. Dean is a young American with liberal and academic inclinations who tries to restrain the gang and is

71

subsequently knocked out; towards the end, he makes a speech in support of self-respect, self-discipline, love, peace and security.

Readers who have experience of acting exercises will not be surprised to learn that Ann Jellicoe wrote the play while working as a director and teacher of acting. While critics have been quick to note the verbal gymnastics, physical ones are equally prominent. Indeed the author herself has claimed that 'nothing is put into words that cannot be shown in action'. The characters hunt one another, dance, disguise themselves, pretend to be musical instruments. Patty is given a home perm while other characters chant the instructions and turn the process into a mock ritual.

The various actions have been given unity by the author's need to shape the play like a musical composition in three parts and — as the author came to recognise when revising the text some years later — by reference to an old myth about a man castrating himself because he was rejected by his mother.

When first performed *The Sport of My Mad Mother* had only a moderate success, but it was recognised as the British play-text which went furthest, at that time, towards the ideal of 'total theatre' associated with the writings of Antonin Artaud (French actor-director, 1896—1948). This reputation and the lively good spirits with which the subject of teenage restlessness and violence is treated have ensured that it has been performed very frequently outside the professional theatre.

PETER NICHOLS   Privates on Parade
b. 1927   *London, 1977*

'As a piece of comic engineering, one must salute the in-
genuity that could construct such a play in the 1970s,'
wrote Charles Marowitz of the first performance of Peter
Nichols' play about a troupe of variety performers in
the army in 1948: 'although it is not uncritical of those
halcyon years, it is palpably affectionate about them,
and to encounter a play motivated by affection rather
than social loathing or class prejudice is itself a rarity
in these days.'

The settings for *Privates on Parade* alternate as front-
cloth and full-stage, in the manner of variety theatre. Between many of the scenes a character turns to address the
audience directly, commenting on what is afoot or filling
out the narrative. Some episodes are excerpts from shows
given by SADUSEA (Song And Dance Unit South East
Asia); others are written so that an audience hardly knows
if it is watching 'performances' or off-stage 'reality'. The
leader of the troupe is Captain Terri Dennis who appears
in a variety of costumes as Noël Coward, Marlene Dietrich,
Carmen Miranda, Vera Lynn, a matelot and a smooth
compère.

But the play is more than a recreation of second-rate
entertainments for the forces in Malaysia. Army routines
and attitudes are mocked, while under-cover Chinese com-
munists watch over the proceedings silently and collude
with a corrupt Sergeant Major. When SADUSEA travels
into the jungle — the train journey is staged as a music,
dance and patter routine — a network of terrorists closes
around the unbelligerent *artistes*, so that their climactic
performances are played as if to a hall packed with un-

73

responsive Gurkas who know no English, and the event is disrupted by violence and bloodshed.

Another strand in the play presents the story of Steven Flowers, a new member of SADUSEA who views everything with the earnestness of a school-teacher-to-be and the inexperience of a schoolboy from 56 Fernleaze Crescent, Swindon. A local girl, half Indian and half Welsh, teaches him about sex and then the Emergency that is declared in Malaya teaches him about colonialism and violence. He also discovers what it is like to be promoted by the Major who sees in him the son he had never had. Steve is one of the main critical voices in the play, but he is himself wide-open to criticism, and this is nailed to him by almost everybody he meets — notably by Terri Dennis whose code of honour Steve is on the point of breaking.

Pastiche lyrics, slick changes from one style to another, nine robustly individualised characters — together with two silent and inscrutable Chinese — and the sheer invention, that keeps burlesque, comedy, variety, narrative, suspense and political comment in prodigal supply, together account for the unusual and unforced ebullience of this play.

Peter Nichols is a comic writer without pretensions: 'I just don't see things tragically,' he says, 'my characters meet adversity cheerfully and humorously, as I try to do.' He also stays close to life, despite the vivacity and wit of his plays: 'I can only write dialogue when I hear people's voices in my mind; my writing is not really creative — it comes from memory and imitation; I've always been a good mimic.'

See also p. 27.

What the Butler Saw
London, 1969

Farce often seems like life in a lucid nightmare or madhouse. Purposes and identities are mistaken, clothes removed and exchanged, pace speeded-up astonishingly, with unlikely entries, precipitate exits, drawn curtains, slammed doors, brandished pistols and, in more recent times, naked bodies. In order to survive, characters are forced to invent — and, often, to believe — the most unlikely stories or rationalisations. All this Joe Orton took as an image of life itself and crammed every available trick into *What the Butler Saw*. He accentuated the alarming nature of this absurdity by setting the play in a private clinic for the insane. The attitudes and jargon of mental care are mixed bewilderingly with those of sexual innuendo when the resident psychiatrist, Dr Prentice, interviews a prospective secretary, Geraldine Bartlett; and when Mrs Prentice arrives with a page boy, Nicholas Beckett, who has photographs of their encounter in a linen cupboard at the Station Hotel. As John Lahr says, 'Torture, nymphomania, transvestism, incest, blackmail, bribery parade across the stage while psychoanalytic prattle twists experience into meanings all its own.' Official surveillance and investigation are further ingredients with the arrivals of Dr Rance to report on Dr Prentice for the Home Office and of Police Sergeant March to search for the private parts of Sir Winston Churchill which are said to have been in the possession of Geraldine's recently deceased step-mother.

The first performance of *What the Butler Saw* baffled and outraged most of its critics, but John Russell Taylor was to write later that Orton's was 'the most glittering artificial comedy in English since Congreve' (1670–1729).

Gareth Lloyd Evans comments that 'language itself, seeming so rational, but with serpents of contradiction, madness, irrelevance, farce, despair lurking beneath, is one of the most vital characters of the play. . . . Orton takes the implications of some of his comic situations and characters further than Congreve — into regions where a fierce moral judgement has to be made by the audience upon the nature of what is happening and what is being said. To this extent Orton's comedy is "black"; but it is essentially, like Congreve's, a verbal comedy.'

Orton's dialogue is formally poised — he compiled lists of assiduously polished jokes for insertion into future work — so that words provide precise points in the encounters, no matter how headlong or aggressive the action becomes.

In the final moments a siren wails and metal grills cover every exit. While the consulting room is lit only by a bloody sunset, the characters are trapped and an artificial resolution is provided: Geraldine and Nicholas are revealed as the twin children of the Prentices, conceived before their marriage in the linen cupboard of the Station Hotel, and Winston Churchill's missing part is discovered in a box that Geraldine had brought on stage at the very beginning. Charged full of egotistical and opportunistic energy, the characters are content, for the moment, to conform and to put on their clothes and face the world. Words from *The Revenger's Tragedy* (*c.* 1606), prefixed to Orton's published text, suggest a possible response for the audience:

> Surely we're all mad people, and they
> Whom we think are, are not.

See also pp. 32–3.

Inadmissable Evidence
London, 1965

At the start of the play, the Royal Coat of Arms is high above the stage. Below it sits one of Her Majesty's Judges and downstage, in the prisoner's dock, is Bill Maitland, a solicitor specializing in divorce cases. He is the hero and will be continuously at the centre of attention. At this time the characters and dialogue have a strange inertia, with the blur and movement of a dream.

The setting and style soon change however, and the play proceeds to show the solicitor's office and the routines of professional life. Only, for Maitland, the dream retains a hold, and for him reality is a kind of nightmare. He judges the world around him and finds it vulgar and depressing; and he senses that he, himself, is judged and, ultimately, condemned.

John Osborne represents this in his play by having the Judge and Clerk of Court take off their wigs and gowns to become Hudson and Jones, the Managing Clerk and his assistant in Maitland's office. Later the actor playing Jones goes off-stage to return as Mr Maples, a young client charged with indecent assault; and the actress playing Mrs Garnsey reappears as two other clients. These scenes are handled so that the audience shares Maitland's sense of finding his own problems wherever he turns; in talking to everyone — his clerks, secretary and telephonist, his mistress and young daughter, and, off-stage on the 'phone, his wife — Maitland projects his own thoughts into theirs and finds his own inadequacies ever present before him. At times the audience cannot know whether he is aware of the person to whom he is talking, or if he is simply tormenting himself or seeking to control his own unappeased thoughts and feelings.

Maitland says and does many things that are self-regarding, or helplessly angry or fearful, or, by ordinary standards, corrupt and deceitful, but nevertheless he gains sympathy for his pain and for his dogged and corrosively witty pursuit of a life of power, truth and generosity of spirit, a life that would transcend everything he is able to achieve. As Katherine Worth says, 'the temperament that cuts him off from other people and shuts him in on himself is the same temperament that keeps him open in imaginative feeling.'

Bill Maitland has the flailing and uncertain eloquence of Samuel Beckett's characters (see pp. 9—11) who represent twentieth-century Man's attempt to rethink, escape or accept his awareness of himself. But Osborne has anchored his fiction in the details of an individual life, full of people and places, and precisely remembered pleasures and horrors. Besides Maitland does plead 'Not Guilty', even as he knows that little choice is involved and that he cannot escape and cannot begin again.

Inadmissable Evidence is a modern tragedy, a British equivalent to the American *Death of a Salesman* (1949) by Arthur Miller. No actual death is shown, but Maitland's slow defeat is realised in painful detail, until he sits waiting for the Law Society to take charge of him. The action of this play is the slow attrition of its hero, pursued from within and without, fighting for hope beyond hope and beyond his own self-lacerating sense of absurdity and loss, wishing that he were older than his thirty-nine years so that he would have less to 'find out'.

All critics agree that the quality of the central performance, first created by Nicol Williamson, is crucial for the success of this play.

See also pp. 4—5 and 25.

HAROLD PINTER   The Homecoming
b. 1930   London, 1965

Unexpectedly Teddy comes back from the United States
to his old home in North London to visit his widowed
father, Max, his uncle Sam and two younger brothers,
Lenny and Joey. Just before the end of the play, he leaves
to return to his children and his job as Professor of Philosophy, but Ruth, his wife, stays on in the old home with
the family she has never met before. Sam has a heart
attack having told the family that a man called MacGregor
had 'had' their mother, Jesse, years ago in the back of his
taxi; he lies on the floor as if dead. For all the characters
truths come home, and in the silence of the play's last
moments a new home-circle is established centred on
Ruth: Max is the last to speak having crawled towards her
on the floor and around Sam's body; Joey kneels with his
head in her lap; and Lenny stands watching.

This basic story is presented in *The Homecoming* with a
ruthless clarity, with imaginative reach, cutting words,
weighty silences, decisive movements and, above all, with
an unprecedented objectivity that is given no underpinning
by authorial comment or talk about meaning. As a result,
an audience is caught up in the fiction and finds its own
fears and impulses mirrored in those of the characters;
often it may only half-guess at the significance of a speech
or action, but it is engaged in the play, exploring its sug-
gestions and sharing its encounters in a manner not unlike
that of the author when he wrote it or the actors when
they rehearsed it.

The setting establishes a double reality. A large living-
room has had the wall removed that once separated it from
a hallway with front door and staircase to the bedrooms.

79

The archway is square, giving more vertical emphasis than the width of the theatre's proscenium within which the room is set. It acts like a frame within a frame, and accentuates the 'two large armchairs' in contrast to 'odd tables, chairs' and to some large pieces of furniture which are placed on either side. The realistic living-room is effectually a throne-room, at first for Max and then for Ruth: he is a surly, bullying monarch but, once she has taken 'her chair', she has little to say and is almost unmoving.

Each character has resources that the others cannot emulate. Lenny tells violent autobiographical stories with unnerving coolness and precision. Joey is training as a boxer. Max lays about him with a stick and does the cooking for the household; both he and Sam talk about the family's past, but Sam has his own life as a chauffeur outside the home. The men find that Ruth is undeniably attractive and she knows how to use this power; with Teddy, who is disconcertingly independent in mind and clear in whatever he says, she has learnt how to retain her own initiative. All of them lie habitually, disguising their true intentions, but each of them wants to be believed and to find some alternative to isolation. All take strong action to assert themselves over others and all fail to do so. Only Teddy breaks away to other engagements and only Ruth finds a new power and ease by submitting, under her own precise conditions, to an unlikely future that others have planned for her.

The action is sometimes swift, but the predominant effect is of slow motion. Each encounter takes its own time for the characters to engage and disengage, for small actions or short phrases to register and to imply, or to gather, meanings and associations. So the second Act opens unhurriedly with the silent lighting of cigars and serving of coffee; this is followed by a savouring of simple-sounding compliments that suggest shifts of consciousness and power.

The play is written so that an audience becomes attuned to its style of presentation. Pinter has said nothing explicit about the basis of family life, about the role of a woman or mother or child, or about the relative powers of intelligence, physical strength and sexuality, or about the dangers of isolation and fear, but an audience senses how these and other elements of living operate within the encounters of daily life, and this registers with the wonder of a new discovery.

See also pp. 12–16.

STEPHEN POLIAKOFF
b. 1952

City Sugar
London, 1975

City Sugar is set in and around a local radio station, where Leonard Brazil, the disc jockey, broadcasts messages to his fans. The heat, routine, skill, hasty improvisation and strongly projected egos are all there; the very 'smell' of the studio is realised through many small, authentic details of dialogue and action.

The DJ is an ambitious man who is on the point of moving from provincial Leicester to London and Capital Radio. He is adept in the language of pop-culture and instant hits and manipulates easily all the images that jostle each other in the minds of his unseen audiences. But he is also self-critical: he has been a school teacher and doubts whether his present work is achieving anything comparable to his earlier vocation. When he does decide to go to London, at the end of the play, Leonard's whole lifetime is wide open to view, and at risk.

The action is complicated by 'Competition Week' at Radio Leicester. As the phone-in starts, the way that Nicola Davies says her name sparks off Leonard's curiosity; he needs to know what this anonymous voice that gives nothing away could possibly conceal. He chooses Nicola as a finalist so that she comes to the studio, where Leonard goads her into speaking without reserve. Asked to talk against the clock about the last pop concert she had attended her rising hatred and sense of emptiness become as shockingly evident as her helplessness. Leonard awards her second prize and, when they are left alone together, he cannot stop himself asking what she thought of the competition. Even when he takes hold of her arm, she has nothing to say, beyond that she doesn't want to say anything. The play is over except for a scene in the supermarket where Nicola works, and in which she starts chucking all the frozen food out of the freezer cabinets, and another scene in the studio in which Leonard collects himself and makes his farewell to Leicester — he is going to take the job in London.

The energy of the writing — its quick, nervous rhythms, neatly controlled and unexpected climaxes, tangible and witty images — together with the cunning shape of the play and the committed performances which the text requires, ensure that audiences share the tense climax fully and with thrilling immediacy. What Michael Coveney calls the 'jagged intensity' of the play catches attention from the start, and then a deeper understanding is developed progressively until it encompasses and probes the lives of the two main characters.

See also pp. 39—40.

DAVID RUDKIN   Ashes
b. 1936   *London, 1973*

Ashes is an intimate play for an intimate theatre: two
characters are kept in close focus, while ten subsidiary
parts are performed by two further actors. But these
minimal means present what would never have been put on
stage in previous ages: the official, social, medical, private
and physical story of a couple who find that they cannot
have children. The first Part starts with deep rhythmic
breathing and intimate bed-talk, and then proceeds through
medical investigations, tests, and vigilance to eventual
pregnancy; Part II takes the story through new social encounters to pain and miscarriage; Part III shows the couple
attempting unsuccessfully to adopt a baby, reacting to the
death of an uncle in Northern Ireland, and realising, in the
last silent moment, that they are alone and have a life to
make together.

David Rudkin draws the audience into the inner consciousness of Colin and Anne, by soliloquy, sudden shifts
of consciousness, stumbling repetitions, wild cries and
careful, physical actions. Stage-directions give precise
indications of tone, facial expression and bodily reaction.
An introductory note prescribes that the indignities to
which Colin and Anne submit themselves during medical
examinations must be acted without any exaggeration so
that the audience may share them, wryly perhaps, as facts;
if these activities cause laughter, the actors should rebuke
the audience by their stillness. Rudkin also specifies that
the whole play should be played without interval and last
no longer than one hundred minutes.

Although its means are small and its subject personal
and domestic, this is never a petty play. In other works,

83

Rudkin has written on a huge scale: *Afore Night Come* (1962) is about a ritual murder in a rural community and his *Sons of Light* (1976) is an apocalyptic vision. He has adapted Euripedes, translated the libretto of Schoenberg's opera *Moses and Aaron*, and written for both opera and ballet. Although Rudkin has narrowed his focus in *Ashes*, his imaginative reach and intellectual concerns are undiminished. Both Colin and Anne are teachers, responsible and articulate, so he can describe terrorism in Ireland with understanding of historical and political forces; and he has been a dramatist and she an actress, so both are able to present themselves deftly and inventively. Sometimes the action is backed by music — specific compositions by Mahler, Schubert and Vaughan Williams, and unspecified and unskilled piano exercises — and, when he believes he is about to become a father, Colin quotes from the mystical poet, Thomas Traherne (?1637—1674).

Ashes has an 'overwhelming eloquence', as Peter Ansorge said when it was first performed. This power derives from economy and also from a wide range of styles that embraces operatic resonance, caricature simplicity, scientific statement and televisual physical intimacy. When Colin travels in an ambulance with Anne — very simply represented on stage — he crouches beside her as she lies in pain so that his face is close to hers, and then he addresses the audience directly: her tears, her swollen, quivering eyes and slack, helpless jaw are all registered, indelibly, by his words. A few minutes after this, Colin stands beside Anne in hospital with a bunch of wild flowers in his hand; he gives them to her and she makes no response. At other times Rudkin encourages the audience to feel superior to the play or to laugh at official pretensions and incapacity.

Amadeus

London, 1979

The play opens with whispers heard from around the darkened theatre, savage whispers among which 'Salieri!' and 'Assassin!' can be distinguished. As the light grows, various people are seen scurrying across the stage and speaking urgently. A silent old man in a wheelchair with his back to the audience is at last identified as Antonio Salieri, the composer who claims that he poisoned his rival, the younger Mozart, some thirty years earlier. The anonymous rumour-mongers ask why he should have done such a thing and the play proper is about to begin, in the small hours of a November morning in 1823. Salieri turns to stare at members of the audience and then tells his story.

Peter Shaffer has used theatrical artifice openly and liberally. Salieri goes to a forte-piano to accompany his cracked voice in an operatic invocation of the audience. He breaks off for a mocking reference to Rossini and then, by way of an admission of his love of sweet cakes, he tells of his birth and early desire for fame. A moment later he is kneeling, to show how, as a child, he had made a compact with God, promising to be virtuous in return for fame as a composer. Then, after a brief account of Wolfgang Amadeus Mozart touring Europe as an infant prodigy, Salieri announces his last composition, entitled 'The Death of Mozart, or Did I Do It?' He bows deeply to the audience, unbuttons his dressing gown and stands erect again as a young man, finely dressed as a successful composer of the seventeen-eighties, and the audience begins to hear music. The setting changes frequently and the story unfolds easily. More characters are introduced: the Emperor Joseph II and his officials, Salieri's wife and his favourite pupil and, before too long, Mozart, aged twenty-five, making his entrance to the Emperor's court. Now the play is accompanied by timely quotations from Mozart's glorious and irresistible music, but Shaffer off-sets this by portraying the composer as excitable, giggling and bursting with vanity and petulance, playing rowdy games and uttering silly obscenities with Constanze Weber, who later becomes his wife.

The first Act ends with Salieri falling senseless on the ground after hearing a full flood of music from Mozart's *Kyrie* in the C Minor Mass: he knows that he is forever mediocre and calls God his enemy for giving his splendid gift to the spiteful, sniggering, conceited and infantile Mozart. He swears to block God's purposes on earth.

The second Act continues the narrative of Mozart's life and begins the melodrama of Salieri's revenge. As Mozart's music becomes ever more wonderful, Salieri schemes to ensure that it is not performed and that its composer is not honoured or paid. Finally Salieri dresses up like the masked figure which haunts the impoverished Mozart in his frenzied dreams, and he demands his death.

After Mozart's painful and agonized death, the story has a final twist. Thirty years later Salieri is shown as he was at the beginning of the play: he is no longer in favour himself, and he knows that Mozart has gained a posthumous fame he can never equal. In revenge for this he attempts suicide, leaving a statement informing the world that he has poisoned Mozart: because he will not be remembered for creating absolute beauty, he is determined to be remembered for murdering the man who could. But at once voices are heard saying that Salieri failed to kill himself and that no-one in the world believes his story: Salieri who would not be mocked by God is mocked at the last by fellow men. He looks out into the theatre and addresses all the mediocrities who are there, absolving them as Mozart's music yet again fills the theatre.

With clear narrative and theatrical showmanship, Peter
Shaffer leads an audience through a parable: a zealous and
intelligent man is destroyed by an obsession with fame and
a sense of his own inadequacies. *Amadeus* is a bold play
that grips its audience; its strange theme is entirely intel-
ligible and is given credibility by marvellous music.

See also pp. 29—30.

TOM STOPPARD	Jumpers
b. 1937	*London, 1972*

Jumpers is 'something unique in theatre', says Kenneth
Tynan: 'a farce whose main purpose is to affirm the
existence of God.'

It is set in Britain of the future: the Radical Liberals
have just won absolute power, and their victory procession
and show of military strength are heard off-stage. A Coda
to the play's two Acts shows the atheist Archbishop of
Canterbury being accused of not pacifying the crowds who
weep in his garden at Lambeth and, then, being shot. Both
state and university are run by Sir Archibald Jumper, who
has degrees in medicine, philosophy, literature and law,
together with diplomas in psychiatry and gymnastics; he
also has a pack of obedient acrobats who double as profes-
sors of philosophy and deal efficiently with the corpses of
assassination victims. But the substance of the play is less
apocalyptic: starting after a Rad-Lib. celebration party
which he finds too noisy, Professor George Moore tries to
dictate and improvise a lecture due to be given that night
at the annual symposium on the subject 'Man — good, bad

or indifferent?' George assembles statements, arguments, analogues, references, demonstrations, parables, paradoxes, metaphors, non-sequiturs, mishaps and dead-ends, and he returns again and again to his first question: 'Is God?' He is irrational, resourceful, tireless, hesitant, impulsive, and, when roused, assertive. Here the futuristic farce gives way to an astonishing portrait of a man daring to use words — words which constantly betray, rather than express, his meaning. He is attempting to give himself some confidence in existence and this, for him, is a matter of universal import, far more demanding than national or international politics.

George is at almost every possible disadvantage. He is *not* the George Moore who wrote *Principia Ethica* and died in 1958. He has a totally silent but supercilious secretary. He knows that argument with a school of rival academics is like trying to construct a Gothic arch out of junket. He is married to Dotty Moore, a super-sexy singing-star who has had a break-down the very moment she achieved success and is now attempting a come-back; meanwhile she seems, occasionally, to enjoy life as Sir Archibald's mistress. 'Why did she marry *him*?' is the question to which George has had to become inured. He discovers that the corpse of McFee, Professor of Logic, is in his wife's bedroom, and also that she has caused the death of the pet goldfish. A little later he is appalled when it seems that he has shot his own pet hare and, at the same time, crushed to death his pet tortoise. Finally George is not brave: hearing a cry for help in the nightmare coda, he answers only with an update of the parable of the Good Samaritan.

Through all this George perseveres until, in the last moments, words fail him in the middle of citing the testimony of other witnesses, including 'Jesus Moore' and a lately deceased friend who was 'as innocent as a rainbow'. Sir Archie takes over then with easy optimism and Dotty sings, without music, about the Moon that obsesses her.

Jumpers is a farce full of words and a play built upon ideas: but equally necessary to its success, as Tom Stoppard says, is a 'more overt "theatricality" ' — gunshots, music, dance, acrobatics, visual jokes, revolving scenery, multiple doors, and a large-scale television screen on which Dotty watches the landing of two men on the moon. The uneasy yoking together of these two opposites helps to give that sense of precarious affirmation which is a constant factor in Stoppard's plays.

See also pp. 27—9.

DAVID STOREY
b. 1933

Early Days
London, 1980

Sir Richard Kitchen, an elderly man in summer clothes, walks on stage speaking a very few words to himself, and moving his hands. He relaxes, glances around and then reminisces about a day in childhood when he stood alone beneath a high and narrow footbridge near the sea. At the end of the play's four short scenes — each one shorter than its predecessor, so that the first is only nineteen pages in print and the last only a few lines over three — Kitchen is again on stage alone, and again speaking about the bridge; but now he says that he had feared it would fall and that strange faces were staring down at him. After this he speaks his wife's name, Ellen, and then turns and says it again. Now the light on him, which has been gathering strength while the rest of the stage has grown darker, is extinguished suddenly.

Early Days is composed like a poem that unfolds in a measured way and holds every moment of clarity together. The audience learns a lot about Kitchen and something about his daughter and son-in-law, his grand-daughter and her fiance, and other members of the household, but plot is slight and situation suggested rather than realised: the various incidents scarcely disturb the basically slow rhythm and low key; no theme is ever stated in words. The action 'does not push the characters to the edge of desperation', as Michael Billington says, but the play 'has the insidious simplicity of a piano piece by Satie or a Wordsworth lyrical ballad'.

David Storey has said that he works best 'if I don't intrude upon the material and if it makes its own shape . . . which is integral to the . . . emotional content of the play or the novel or the poem.' Here the basic material is the character, Kitchen. He was written for Sir Ralph Richardson and when Sir Ralph did create the role some years after composition, the critics found they could not disentangle his achievement and Storey's; most of them praising the actor rather than the dramatist.

The memory of the bridge is only one facet of the character that keeps being repeated and questioned: Did one speech destroy his promising political career? Is he thinking of defecting to the USSR? Does he believe that his daughter should kill her husband? How long has he got to live? Is he mad or sane, or is he pretending to be mad, and sometimes profound, to confuse his family and resist their surveillance? On the other hand, he does urinate in public in the village; his son's ansafone does record his scurrilous messages; he has been ordered not to drink; he is watched almost every minute; and he meddles endlessly and unnecessarily in other people's lives. Most certainly his mind goes back to his early days with a sense of wonder, and to his wife, whom he has almost certainly ill-treated.

The central character holds centre-stage — he is there, available for scrutiny — and yet he is mysterious. The man is haunted, and the whole play with him: from behind the obvious puzzles, an incipient violence seems ready to break out, and a simple sweetness and sense of loving seem to have left some relics.

See also p. 6.

ARNOLD WESKER   Roots
b. 1932   *Coventry and London, 1959*

'Let the Battle Commence' was the title of an article by Arnold Wesker in *Encore*, a theatre journal, in 1958, a year before *Roots* was first performed. Drama was for him 'a tool, equipment for the enjoyment of living, for its better understanding'. He announced, quite frankly, 'I want to teach'.

The central character of this play, Beatie Bryant, has been taught by Ronnie, someone who never appears although his arrival is prepared for throughout the three Acts. He has been invited to meet Beatie's family, or as many of them as can be persuaded to sit down together, for high tea. She expects to be marrying him, but a letter arrives, and is read out, which tells her that he has decided, after three years, that this would not work. Ronnie has taught Beatie his own opinions about society, politics, culture; he wants the best things in life — dignity, co-operation, happiness — and Beatie, returning from London to rural Norfolk, can quote her master on almost any occasion. The letter of rejection also announces that he finds his own ideas to be useless and romantic. Everything seems in ruin; Beatie's earlier relapses into reading comics and acquiescence now seem to have been prophetic and her reformation only surface deep. But after she has turned her anger towards her mother and been slapped in the face for it, Beatie finds words to castigate the empty and stubborn life from which she needs to escape: she has got no tools for living, she says, and no roots that take life from anything of lasting worth. Confessing this, she ends the play in a blaze of triumph: in passionate rhetoric, which draws on her own experience and not on books or lessons, she denounces meaningless work and the entertainment offered to the masses by commercial entrepreneurs. She stands on her own two feet, literally and metaphorically, while the family start on the food, eating mindlessly.

This strong final curtain reveals a transformed Beatie and it is the clinching moment of what Wesker called 'a theatrical demonstration' of the bankruptcy of a life that submits to unrewarding labour, isolation and ignorance. As Glenda Leeming and Simon Trussler point out, this rural community is presented in 'deliberately anti-romantic terms'. The Bryants live with so little intensity that the stage-action is often routine and the dialogue perfunctory. Silences are not used here so that they sharpen attention on particular words or gestures which reveal hidden involvement, as in plays by Harold Pinter; and they are not still centres of dramatic conflict, as in plays by John Osborne. Speaking or not, these characters keep a low tension most of the time. Except for Beatie and the old and wayward Stan Mann, who dies off-stage during the second Act, they show energy only by fits and starts, or by retreating to entrenched positions of aggression or withdrawal. Step by step Wesker's demonstration of a rural community is filled out. The audience might well lose interest if Beatie were not there, alive and unsettled until she finds her confidence.

See also pp. 5–6.

Veterans

At the beginning two old men sit in two deck chairs. The curtain rises and falls twice before a word is spoken, and while it is down the audience is presented with military music, gunfire, the din of battle and credit-titles for a film about the Indian Mutiny. On the second rise, the old men are seen to be veteran actors in costume: Sir Geoffrey Kendle, or 'Sir G', and Mr Laurence D'Orsay, or 'Dotty'. When it rises for the third time, they have been joined by a young woman and Sir G goes off to see what is what. Only on a fourth rise, does the play get under way with talk of the film that is being made in Turkey.

The main characters are the two veterans, a young star uncertain of his reputation, an actress married to Dotty, a cook, an electrician, and the Director of the film, Trevor Hollingshead. In the second Act, the setting changes to the place where the film is being shot, but the most that is shown of film-making is Sir G standing on a wooden box and rehearsing a long speech. It is an account of a nightmare of battle and massacre at the gates of Cawnpore, and expresses moral concern as well as savage barbarism. Spoken by Sir John Gielgud in the first production of *Veterans*, the solo performance held attention as in a vice: a great actor caught in the middle of a mishandled epic, eloquence contrasted with so much polite and vindictive talk, intensity opposed to idleness. An interlude of furious noise follows and then dust is seen to be settling; and Sir G, still on his box, is unable to make contact with anyone. Now he uses his own words and then attempts, in silence, to concentrate himself in readiness to act once more. Then he tries to scramble down from his perch, despite trousers that are too tight.

Charles Wood wrote for Gielgud a part which is both tribute to the actor's professional skill, individuality and integrity and also a display of those 'veteran' qualities in a world of deceit, exploitation, treachery, pretension and absurdity. Ronald Bryden says that 'All the backstage legends of Gielgud's tactlessness are exploited for full risible value. But they're fitted into the framework of a nature in which exquisite politeness is in constant tug-of-war with iron, unbending truth about artistic value. . . . The total impression is of a kind of saint of the theatre.'

This portrait dominates the play, at the risk of action that is too desultory and other characters that either shine only briefly in sharply characterised speech — Rodney the cook and Bernie the electrician — or have to spend most of their time in support of Sir G. But the dialogue is nicely judged; it is printed in short lines that indicate the phrasing and rhythms which control the prose with revealing exactness. Stage-directions also indicate that physical response is sometimes strong and unexpected: Trevor, the young director, grins, laughs brayingly, or fidgets and may seem to be shy; but, in effect, he is shrewd and tough.

Who's Who and Select Bibliography

ANSORGE, Peter
   Author of *Disrupting the Spectacle: Five Years of Experimental and Fringe Theatre* (Pitman, 1975) and sometime editor of *Plays and Players* in which many of his reviews are found.

BARBER, John
   Drama critic of *The Daily Telegraph.*

BIGSLEY, C.W.E.
   Academic and critic; associate editor of the *Contemporary English Drama* volume of *Stratford-upon-Avon Studies* (Arnold, 1981), to which he contributed the long introductory chapter.

BILLINGTON, Michael
   Drama critic of *The Guardian* and author of a book on Acting.

BROOK, Peter
   Associate Director of the Royal Shakespeare Company and Director of the International Centre for Theatre Research, Paris; a play, opera and film director, he is also author of *The Empty Space* (Macgibbon & Kee, 1968).

BRYDEN, Ronald
   Now an academic and previously, until the mid-seventies, drama critic of *The Observer* and then Literary Manager of the Royal Shakespeare Company, when he continued to review occasionally for *Plays and Players.*

COULT, Tony
   Actor and teacher, who wrote the first book-length study of Edward Bond, *The Plays of Edward Bond* (Methuen, 1977).

COVENEY, Michael
   Drama critic for *The Financial Times* and, from 1975 to 1978, editor of *Plays and Players.*

EVANS, Gareth Lloyd
   Academic and drama critic for *The Guardian*; he is author of books on J.B. Priestley, Shakespeare and *The Language of Modern Drama* (Dent, 1977).

HALL, Peter
   Director of the Royal Shakespeare Theatre and then of the

National Theatre; *Director's Theatre*, edited Judith Cook (Harrap, 1974) contains an interview with him.

HAYMAN, Ronald

Author of many short studies of post-war British playwrights (Heinemann Educational Books) and of *British Theatre Since 1955: A Reassessment* (Oxford University Press, 1979); he has also published *Artaud and After, Acting, John Gielgud, The Set-Up: An Anatomy of English Theatre Today*, etc.

HOBSON, Harold

Drama critic of *The Sunday Times* until 1977 and author of volumes of collected criticism and studies of *French Theatre* and *Ralph Richardson*.

HUNT, Albert

Drama teacher, director and critic; he is author of *Hopes for Great Happenings: Alternatives in Education and Theatre* and *Arden: A Study of His Plays* (Eyre Methuen, 1976 and 1974).

LAHR, John

Drama critic for *Village Voice* (New York) and dramaturg; he is author of *Prick Up Your Ears: The Biography of Joe Orton* (Allen Lane, 1978).

LEEMING, Glenda

Author, with Simon Trussler, of *The Plays of Arnold Wesker* (Gollancz, 1971).

MAROWITZ, Charles

Theatre director, author of *Confessions of a Counterfeit Critic, 1958−71* (Eyre Methuen, 1973) and contributor to *Plays and Players* and other journals.

PETER, John

Drama critic and broadcaster.

TAYLOR, John Russell

Author of *Anger and After: A Guide to the New British Drama* and *The Second Wave* (Methuen, 1962 and 1971); he has also contributed Part II ('Dramatists and plays since 1880') to the *Revels History of Drama in English*, vii (Methuen, 1978).

TRUSSLER, Simon

Editor of *Theatre Quarterly*, drama critic of *The Tribune* and author, with Glenda Leeming, of a study of *The Plays of Arnold Wesker* (Gollancz, 1971).

TYNAN, Kenneth

Critic and impressario, and the first Literary Manager of the National Theatre, London: author of *A View of the English Stage, 1944−63* (Davis-Poynter, 1975); his *Show People* (Weidenfeld &

Nicolson, 1980) contains an extensive account of Tom Stoppard.

WARDLE, Irving
Drama critic of *The Times*, London, and author of *The Theatres of George Devine* (Cape, 1978).

WORTH, Katharine J.
Academic and author of *Revolutions in Modern English Drama* (G. Bell & Sons, 1972).

Index to Plays

AC/DC 12
Afore Night Come 84
Alpha Beta 34
Amadeus 30
American Days 39
Ashes 83—4

Bedroom Farce 47—8
Betrayal 16
Bingo 54—6
Birthday Party, The 12
Butley 33—4

Caretaker, The 13—14
Changing Room, The 6
City Sugar 39, 81—2
Cocktail Party, The 3
Collection, The 14—15
Contractor, The 6

Destiny 8
Donkey's Years 61—3

Endgame 51
Entertainer, The 25
Entertaining Mr. Sloane 31
Epsom Downs 57—8
Equus 29—30

Fings Ain't Wot They Used T'Be 26
Flowering Cherry 3, 53

German Skerries 34
Gimme Shelter 39

Happy Days 51—2
Homecoming, The 79—81

Inadmissable Evidence 77—8
Inspector Calls, An 3

Jumpers 87—9

Kitchen, The 5—6

Lear 21
Life Class, The 6
Look Back in Anger 4, 11
Loot 33

Make and Break 34
Man for All Seasons, A 53—4

National Health, The 27
No End of Blame 49—50
No Man's Land 15—16
Norman Conquests, The 36
Not I 51

Oh What a Lovely War 26
Old Country, The 39
Old Times 15
One Way Pendulum 12
Otherwise Engaged 33, 63—4

Party, The 23
Philanthropist, The 35
Play 51
Plenty 22—3
Pope's Wedding, The 19

Privates on Parade 73

Relatively Speaking 35
Romans in Britain, The 23
— Room, The 12
Roots 91—2
Rosencrantz and Guildenstern
    are Dead 27—8
Royal Hunt of the Sun, The 29

Saint's Day 32
Saved 19—20
Separate Tables 3
Serjeant Musgrave's Dance
    17—18
Short, Sharp Knock, A 23—4
Sisterly Feelings 36—7
Sons of Light 84
Sore Throats 23

Sport of My Mad Mother, The
    12, 71—2
Summer Party 39—40

Taste of Honey, A 26, 59—60
Teeth'n'Smiles 69—70
That Good Between Us 23
— Travesties 28—9
Treats 34—5, 67—8

Veterans 93—4
Voyage Round My Father 39

— Waiting for Godot 9—11, 51
Weapons of Happiness 7—8
What the Butler Saw 33, 75—6
Woman, The 20—21
Workhouse Donkey, The 45

Index to Playwrights

Arden, John 17—19, 45—6
Ayckbourn, Alan 35—7, 47—8

Barker, Howard 22, 23, 39,
    49—50
Barnes, Peter 27
Beckett, Samuel 9—11, 12, 15,
    51—2, 78
Behan, Brendan 26
Bennett, Alan 39
Bolt, Robert 3, 53—4
Bond, Edward 19—22, 54—6
Brecht, Bertolt 18—19, 23, 24
Brenton, Howard 7—8, 22,
    23—4, 39, 57—8

Christie, Agatha 13
Coward, Noël 13, 14

Delaney, Shelagh 26, 59—60

Edgar, David 8
Eliot, T. S. 3, 4

Frayn, Michael 34, 61—2

Gems, Jonathan 39
Gray, Simon 33—4, 63—4
Griffiths, Trevor 22, 23, 65—6

Hampton, Christopher 34—5,
    67—8
Hare, David 22—3, 69—70
Holman, Robert 34

Ionesco, Eugene 11

Jellicoe, Ann 12, 27, 71—2

Keefe, Barrie 39, 58

Littlewood, Joan 25—6, 59—60
Livings, Henry 27

Mercer, David 39
Miller, Arthur 78
Mortimer, John 39

Nichols, Peter 27, 73—4
Norman, Barry 26

Orton, Joe 32—3, 75—6
Osborne, John 4—5, 11, 17, 25,
    77—8

Pinter, Harold 12—16, 17, 79—81
Poliakoff, Stephen 39—40, 81—2
Priestley, J. B. 3

Rattigan, Terence 3
Rudkin, David 83—4

Shaffer, Peter 29—30, 85—7
Simpson, N. F. 12
Stoppard, Tom 27—9, 87—9
Storey, David 6, 89—91

Wesker, Arnold 5—6, 17, 91—2
Whitehead, E. A. 34
Whiting, John 32
Williams, Heathcote 12
Wilson, Snoo 39
Wood, Charles 27, 93—4